# Ready-to-Use
# SELF-ESTEEM
## Activities for Young Children

### Jean R. Feldman, Ph.D

JOSSEY-BASS
A Wiley Imprint
www.josseybass.com

Published by Jossey-Bass
A Wiley Imprint
989 Market Street, San Francisco, CA 94103-1741   www.josseybass.com

Jossey-Bass books and products are available through most bookstores. To contact Jossey-Bass directly call our Customer Care Department within the U.S. at 800-956-7739, outside the U.S. at 317-572-3986 or fax 317-572-4002.

Jossey-Bass also publishes its books in a variety of electronic formats. Some content that appears in print may not be available in electronic books.

**Library of Congress Cataloging-in-Publication Data**
Feldman, Jean R.
  Ready-to-use self-esteem activities for young children / Jean R.
  Feldman : illustrations by Rebecca Feldman Foster.
    p.  cm.
    ISBN 0-87628-886-7 (pbk.)
    1. Self-esteem—Study and teaching  (Early childhood)—Handbooks,
  manuals, etc.   2. Early childhood education—Activity programs.
    I. Title.
LB1117.F34   1997                                            96-46213
370.15'3—dc20

FIRST EDITION
*HB Printing* 10 9 8 7 6 5 4 3

*This book is dedicated to someone who truly sees and believes in the best in others—
my sister, Jann Sikkink.*

# About This Book

One of the most powerful and enduring gifts that teachers and parents can give children is a positive sense of self. Without it, children grow up to be negative, dependent, anxious, withdrawn, underachieving, and more likely to "say yes" to drugs, gangs, and dropping out of school.

To help young children feel good about themselves... develop friendships...deal with feelings...celebrate diversity...and accept changes, here is a remarkable collection of 220 activities and ideas that are not only fun, but also provide countless opportunities to reinforce basic academic skills. Each activity takes a unique three-pronged approach:

- the acquisition of self-esteem for the "head"

- the inspiration to make a difference from the "heart"

- creative ideas, projects, and reproducibles for the "hands"

For easy use, all activities include a purpose, materials, step-by-step directions, and ideas to extend learning, and are organized into the following six sections:

- WONDERFUL ME—a total of 60 activities help children appreciate themselves through songs ("Name Rap"), homemade books ("Who Am I?" Big Book), art projects ("Designer T-Shirt"), and other innovative activities ("Chalk Talk")

- FRIENDS, FRIENDS, FRIENDS—46 cooperative learning projects and activities encourage children to have fun with friends ("Friendship Bubble") and to develop social skills ("Moving and Singing with Friends")

- FEELINGS AND EMOTIONS—35 activities show how to acknowledge emotions ("Expression Headbands") and deal with them in acceptable ways ("We Can Work It Out")

- SAME AND DIFFERENT—children can explore how we alike and different with 34 games ("Pass the Parcel"), recipes (What's Cooking at Your House?), music and crafts activities ("People Collage")

- CHANGES—28 activities covering health and fitness ("Fitness Trail"), safety ("Don't Touch"), and other concerns ("If I Could Change the World") empower children with tools for taking care of themselves in today's world

- PARENT PACK—includes 21 reproducible activities for parents to do with their children at home ("Positive Partnerships," "Homework Task Cards," "Who Is My Teacher?")

Teachers need to enhance the whole child emotionally as well as intellectually, physically, and socially to achieve his or her full potential. Although many teachers support this principle, there is very little practical material available to help them nurture emotional development in the classroom. *Ready-to-Use Self Esteem Activities for Young Children* attempts to fill that void.

*Jean R. Feldman*

# About the Author

JEAN R. FELDMAN has been a teacher in the Atlanta area for over 25 years. Currently she is an instructor in the Early Childhood Department of DeKalb Technical Institute. Dr. Feldman has a B.A. from the University of Georgia, a D.A.S.T. from Emory University, and a M.A. and Ph.D. from Georgia State University. She is a member of the National Association for the Education of Young Children, Georgia Association for Young Children, and the Georgia Preschool Association.

Dr. Feldman presents to professional groups across the country, and serves on the board of several organizations. She is the author of three books published by The Center for Applied Research in Education: *A Survival Guide for the Preschool Teacher* (1991), *Complete Handbook of Indoor and Outdoor Games and Activities for Young Children* (1994), and *Science Surprises! Ready-to-Use Experiments & Activities for Young Learners* (1995), as well as the author of *Kids' Atlanta* and other materials for teachers.

She is married and has two children and a dog.

# Why Self-Esteem Is Important

Self-esteem includes all the feelings we have about ourselves, and what we believe about ourselves affects everything we do in life. Self-esteem is complex, changing, and intricately interwoven into who we are. One aspect of self-esteem is self-acceptance. This refers to knowing yourself, having a realistic view of yourself, as well as being comfortable with yourself. Self-worth, or feeling loved and lovable, is another dimension of self-esteem. Successful experiences in life influence self-efficacy, or the belief that you have the skills to deal with life. Another component of "self" is self-respect, for only when you respect yourself can you reach out to others with respect and acceptance. In addition, there is self-confidence, which enables you to believe in yourself and try new things.

It is important not to confuse a healthy self-esteem with self-centeredness. Rather, positive feelings of self enable us to reach our potential, set goals, cope with problems, relate to others, take risks, contribute to society, and become happy, self-fulfilled adults.

Children are not born with a self-esteem, but their esteem will constantly grow and change throughout their lifetime. Self-esteem develops from the child's experiences and how others react to them. If the child has successful experiences and feedback that says, "You're great!" then esteem increases. If the child has failures and negative reactions from others, then esteem decreases. Although self-esteem is not the outcome of a single success, comment, or learning activity, it is a combination of a myriad of experiences, interactions, and feedback from others. Life experiences will not be all positive or negative, but certainly children need many more positive encounters than negative ones to develop a positive sense of self. The significance of nurturing children's self-esteem when they are young is emphasized by the research that suggests esteem is fairly defined by age eight.

Parents, siblings, friends, and teachers all have a profound impact on the development of self-esteem. The way society views the child will also influence the way the child views himself or herself. Clearly, all children, regardless of sex, race, culture, or ability, need unconditional love and assurance from others that they are loved for who they are and *not* what they do or accomplish.

Physical appearance, social acceptance, academic ability, physical prowess, artistic talent, as well as behavior, contribute to children's sense of self in the school setting. But self-esteem is more than being the most attractive, smartest, or talented athlete in the classroom. It's a sense of well-being that radiates from the child. Children with *high* self-esteem are often:

optimistic and enthusiastic about life

confident

friendly, interested in others, and mannerly

happy and have a sense of humor

willing to take risks and try new things

able to set goals and can delay gratification

adaptable and flexible

independent and self-directed

successful and show personal pride in their work

responsible and follow through on tasks

empathetic and concerned about others

cooperative

problem solvers

assertive and express opinions

On the other hand, children with *low* esteem may exhibit these characteristics:

fearful and afraid to try new things

moody, negative

insecure

selfish

underachiever

stressed

complainer and blames others

aggressive, angry

aloof and has trouble getting along with others

submissive, follower

belittles self

needs constant reinforcement

It is no surprise that children with high esteem are more attractive to peers and teachers. They are the team players, leaders, and the type of person everyone wants for a friend. Unfortunately, children with a poor self-esteem are more likely to drop out of school, join gangs, or find comfort in drugs and alcohol. It becomes a self-fulfilling prophecy that impacts individuals as well as society as a whole.

## *The Role of the Teacher*

As educators committed to the whole child, it is critical that you do as much as possible to enhance each child's self-esteem. Rather than a single teaching style, there are many strategies you can utilize to help accomplish this goal.

1. Accept children for who they are and what they are. Your acceptance will lead to feelings of self-acceptance in the child.

2. Treat children as individuals. Cherish their differences and don't compare them.

3. Use children's names frequently. Become familiar with their life outside of school by talking about their siblings, pets, hobbies, etc.

4. Respect children, their families, and their culture.

5. Recognize that there are many ways for children to be talented other than an IQ score.

6. Help children see that they are multi-dimensional. "I'm good at _____, but I need to work on _____."

7. Children tell us things by their behavior, so become a "child observer." Be sensitive to their reactions and comments during the school day.

8. Know what your students are developmentally capable of. Plan a program in which each child can be successful.

9. Empower children by giving them choices.

10. Encourage children to be independent, accept responsibilities, and follow through on tasks.

11. Set clear rules and expectations for behavior. Studies suggest that when children have boundaries and know what is expected of them, they will develop higher self-esteem.

12. Be fair and consistent. Instead of punishment, help children learn to deal with the consequences of their behavior.

13. Follow a schedule and routine so children know what to expect.

14. Provide children with opportunities to vent their energy and emotions with exercise breaks and outdoor play.

15. Remember, it's okay to make mistakes. Avoid overreacting when children do something wrong.

16. Don't use labels, such as "slow poke," "messy," or "nosey."

17. Value creativity and originality.

18. Ask open-ended questions and accept divergent answers.

19. Encourage children to be problem-solvers.

20. Be available to children. Try to give them quality time and connect with them on an individual basis.

21. Model a positive self-esteem and try to be optimistic about life.

22. Let the children know you as a real person by sharing your personal life.

23. Keep a sense of humor and laugh often.

24. Take advantage of nonverbal messages with plenty of smiles and pats on the back.

25. Celebrate children's accomplishments. Recall their past successes and comment on how they are growing and changing.

26. Help children set goals and experience delayed gratification.

27. Use encouragement with children, rather than rewards.

28. Let children overhear you making positive comments about them.

There are also constructive communication techniques that will help you foster a healthy esteem in children:

✏ Listen, listen, listen! Listening to children shows that you care and will give you insight into their thoughts and feelings.

✏ Get down to their level when talking to them and look into their eyes.

✏ Accept children's feelings. Let them know that it's okay to be angry, frustrated, or scared.

✏ Use your tone of voice, body language, and facial expressions to communicate with children.

✏ Say what you mean and mean what you say. Use positive speech and state what behavior you expect.

✎  Be specific with praise and criticism. Helpful praise is timely and relates to the behavior. (Don't overly praise or be insincere.) When a child needs to be criticized, separate the child from the deed. Describe exactly what the child did wrong and what should have been done.

In addition to teaching strategies and communication techniques, the learning environment also has a powerful influence on the development of children's self-concept. These guidelines will help you create a classroom where children can experience success and develop a unique sense of self:

1. Use developmentally appropriate activities, and strive for a program that *fits the child.*

2. Arrange the classroom so children can be independent. Place objects at the children's level so they can get materials out and clean up after themselves.

3. Provide learning centers where children can explore and follow their interests.

4. Capitalize on children's different learning styles with a wide variety of activities.

5. Use open-ended materials where children will be challenged, but not overwhelmed.

6. Give children choices.

7. Develop a daily schedule that is balanced with active and quiet times.

8. Program time for play, free exploration, and fun in your school day.

9. Plan different activities so children can work individually, with a few friends, or in a large group.

10. Give children opportunities to work together on projects in small cooperative groups.

11. Provide children with the materials, space, and time to become involved in meaningful learning.

12. Encourage a sense of community by helping all children feel accepted.

13. Reflect diversity with pictures, books, toys, music, art, and objects from different cultures so all children will feel like they belong.

14. Help children take pride in their work by talking about what they do or sharing things they have made.

15. Use a variety of assessment techniques. A portfolio of art projects, writing samples, photos, and anecdotal records will show what children *can* do.

16. Display children's art work, writings, and other projects.

17. Help the children feel safe and protected with a peaceful, non-threatening classroom environment.

18. Keep your door open to welcome families.

19. Involve the children in the community and in service projects.

Remember, in a child-centered classroom, children's self-esteem, as well as academic and social skills, will flourish! To help you create this child-centered classroom, *Ready-to-Use Self-Esteem Activities for Young Children* was written.

This book is a resource of activities and projects that will nurture children's self-esteem. These ideas can be used to develop a unit of study, or they can be integrated into the entire school year. They focus on helping children feel good about themselves, develop friendships, deal with feelings, cherish diversity, and accept changes. These activities are not only fun, but also provide children with many opportunities to reinforce academic skills.

It is true we cannot control outside forces, but we must try—one at a time—to help all children be the best they can be. Life is a journey, and these experiences will give them the courage and strength to cross new bridges as they come to them.

*Jean R. Feldman*

## I BELIEVE

I believe teachers can help children believe in themselves.

I believe teachers can do this by giving children special experiences and memories.

I believe teachers can help children discover their talents and dreams by encouraging them and by providing them with a wide variety of opportunities.

I believe teachers can also give children the skills and desire to make their dreams come true.

I believe teachers can make a difference in the lives of children, and ultimately the world.

I believe in teachers.

# Resources for Teachers

Berne, P., and Savary, L. *Building Self-Esteem in Children.* New York: Continuum Press, 1981.

Briggs, D. *Your Child's Self-Esteem: The Key to Life.* New York: Doubleday, 1970.

Canfield, J., and Well, H. *100 Ways to Enhance Self-Concept in the Classroom.* Englewood Cliffs, NJ: Prentice Hall, 1976.

Coopersmith, S. *The Antecedents of Self-Esteem.* San Francisco: W. H. Freeman, 1967.

Ginott, H. *Between Teachers and Children.* New York: Macmillan, 1972.

Hart, L. *The Winning Family.* New York: Mead & Co., 1987.

Joseph, J. *The Resilient Child.* New York: Plenum Press, 1994.

# Contents

## 3. Feelings and Emotions . . . . . . . . . . . . . . . . . . . . . . . . . . . . . . 127

## 4. Same and Different . . . . . . . . . . . . . . . . . . . . . . . . . . . . . . . . . 173

# 1

# Wonderful Me

The projects in this section will help you celebrate the individual children in your classroom in a variety of creative ways. As children focus on what makes them special, their esteem and confidence will improve. Behavior and interactions with others will also be more positive when children feel accepted and good about themselves.

# "WHO AM I?" BIG BOOK

This project integrates reading skills with positive feelings of self. It also contributes to a sense of belonging to the classroom group.

**You will need:**

one large sheet of 12" × 18" white paper for each student

crayons or markers (body colors)

tape

colored construction paper cut in 8" × 6" rectangles for each sheet of white paper

hole punch

book rings

**Directions:**

1. One at a time, ask children to dictate a riddle about themselves as you write it on the top half of a large sheet of paper. They might give clues about their physical characteristics, family, favorite things to do at school, pets, and so forth. (Older children could write their own riddles.) jljljljl'

2. Tape one side of the colored construction paper to the bottom half of the page as shown. Ask the child to draw a picture of himself or herself under this flap.

3. Make a cover page for the book that says, "Who Am I?" Make a final page that says, "Who are we? We are ___(name)___'s class and we are all friends!"

4. Punch holes in the sides of the pages and put them together with book rings or yarn.

5. Read the book with the class, encouraging them to guess who each friend is.

6. Place the book in your classroom library for children to read over and over again.

**Variations:**

✏ Let children take turns checking out the book and taking it home to share with their families.

✏ Use photographs of the children to make this book.

# MAGIC MIRROR

What a special surprise for children to see that they are the most wonderful thing in the world!

**You will need:**

box with a lid (shoe box or gift box)
ribbon
small mirror
glue

**Directions:**

1. Glue the mirror to the bottom of the box. Put on the lid and wrap a ribbon around it.

2. Gather the children and tell them that the most wonderful thing in the world is in the box. Let them shake the box and guess what it could be.

3. Unwrap the box and pass it around for each child to take a peek. (Tell them to keep it a secret until everyone has had a turn to look.)

4. Ask the children why they are the most wonderful thing in the world.

**Variations:**

- Spray paint the box gold or silver and decorate it with glitter to look like a treasure box.

- Teach the children this poem:

    **Me**

    | | |
    |---|---|
    | I've got ten fingers | (Hold up fingers.) |
    | and I've got ten toes. | (Point to toes.) |
    | I've got two eyes, | (Point to eyes, |
    | a mouth and a nose. | mouth, and nose.) |
    | Put them all together | (Put hands in air.) |
    | and what do you see? | (Put hands on hips.) |
    | Something wonderful, | (Point to self with |
    | and that's ME! | thumbs.) |

- Place many mirrors around the classroom to contribute to children's sense of self. Mirrors can be placed in the dramatic play area or the art center. Or perhaps you could hang a full-length mirror by the door for children to look at themselves as they come and go.

# WANTED POSTERS

Children will identify their personal physical characteristics and other unique qualities with "wanted posters."

**You will need:**      copy of the "wanted poster" on the following page for each child
crayons or markers
scale
tape measure

**Directions:**

1. Ask the children if they've ever seen a wanted poster. Explain that they're going to make a wanted poster for "being good."

2. Have each child draw his or her picture in the middle of the page and fill in his or her name, hair color, and eye color.

3. Let the children weigh and measure each other and fill in the dimensions.

4. Have the children write or dictate their likes and dislikes at the bottom.

**Variations:**

- Play a guessing game where you read the descriptions on the posters without revealing the pictures. Let children guess who fits the different descriptions.

- Cut pieces of corrugated cardboard into shapes resembling wood scraps and mount the posters on them.

- Hang the posters in the classroom or hallway.

- To make posters look like old paper, paint over them with tea or coffee and hang to dry.

- Let children make up advertisements about themselves—"the world's greatest kid."

# WANTED
## for Being Good

Name _____

Nickname _____ Age _____

Hair Color _____ Eye Color _____

Weight _____ Height _____

Likes _____

Dislikes _____

Best Qualities _____

_____

# SUPER STARS

This project will focus on positive characteristics of each child. Your classroom will "shine" with all the stars!

**You will need:**

one sheet of yellow paper for each child

scissors

crayons

hole punch

string

paper clips

star pattern

**Directions:**

1. Make a copy of the "super star" pattern on the following page for each child from yellow paper and let them cut the stars out.

2. Discuss how we all have characteristics that make us unique and special. It may be something we can do well, something we enjoy, or something about our bodies. Let the children share what they consider to be their special characteristics.

3. Ask the children to draw their picture in the middle of the star, then let them dictate their special characteristics for you to write in the points of the star.

4. Encourage the children to share their stars with classmates, then hang them from the ceiling. (To hang from the ceiling, punch a hole in the top point of the star and tie on a piece of string 18" long. Tie a paper clip to the other end of the string and insert the paper clip under a ceiling tile or from the light fixture.)

**Variations:**

✏ Glue a photograph of the child in the middle of the star.

✏ Decorate a door or a bulletin board with the stars.

✏ Have older children write their own sentences about themselves on the points of the star.

# SUPER STARS

# ROLL ON

This is a delightful get-acquainted activity that gives children the opportunity to share personal information with others.

**You will need:** one roll of toilet paper

**Directions:**

1. Have the children sit in a circle. Pass around the toilet paper with the instructions. "Tear off as much as you need."

2. When everyone has taken some toilet paper, explain that they are going to tear off one square at a time. As they do so, they have to tell the group something special about themselves.

3. You demonstrate how to do this by telling your name, something about your family, likes, dislikes, etc., as you remove each section.

4. Go around the circle and let each child tell about himself or herself as he or she tears off the toilet paper.

**Variations:**

- Let the children help themselves to popcorn, snack mix, or small candy. Tell them they must say something about themselves for each piece before eating it.

- Give children yarn and instruct them to cut off a piece. They must introduce themselves to the group as they wind the yarn around their finger.

# "STEP BOOK ABOUT ME"

The "Step Book About Me" encourages children to express their likes, friends, and other special qualities. It also provides children with a simple technique for making homemade books.

**You will need:**
three sheets of white paper for each child
stapler
markers or crayons

**Directions:**

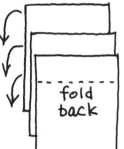

1. Give each child three pieces of paper. Demonstrate how to lay the sheets under each other 1-1/2 inches apart as illustrated.

2. Fold the top of the papers backwards to make six pages. Staple on the top fold.

3. Let the children draw the following pictures on each page:

    | | | |
    |---|---|---|
    | first page | — | name |
    | second page | — | "This is a picture of me." |
    | third page | — | "This is my family." |
    | fourth page | — | "These are my friends." |
    | fifth page | — | "Things I like." |
    | sixth page | — | "The best thing about me." |

4. Place the books in your classroom library for the children to read.

**Variations:**

- Use this as a get-acquainted activity at the beginning of the school year.

- Change pages to include "This is my home," "This is my pet," "This is what I want to be when I grow up," and other personal characteristics.

- Use step books for book reports, writing stories, or for other assignments in the classroom.

- Make step books with fewer or more pages.

# DRIVER'S LICENSE

Children will feel very grown-up with their own driver's license. They will be able to identify their hair color, eye color, name, birthday, and other physical attributes.

**You will need:**

small photo of each child
one copy of the driver's license at the bottom of this page for each child
glue
scale and tape measure
pencils or pens
mirror

**Directions:**

1.  Show the children your driver's license. "Why do adults need a driver's license?" Have the children identify your photograph, name, eye color, and so forth.

2.  Give each child a copy of the license below. Ask them to write their name and glue their photo on the card.

3.  Let each child tell you his or her birthday. Ask the children to look in the mirror and tell you their hair color and eye color.

4.  Weigh and measure the children and record them on their cards.

**Variations:**

- Laminate licenses or cover with clear self-stick vinyl.

- Have children use their driver's license when they want to ride a toy outside.

- Cut heavy cardboard into 8″ × 4″ rectangles and let them make a personalized license plate for their bikes.

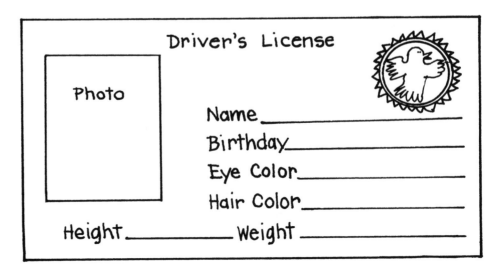

# PICTURE PUPPETS

> These puppets will enhance children's self-esteem and encourage oral language. They can also be used for working out problems and role-playing.

**You will need:**

photo of each child

large craft sticks

scissors

tape

markers

can, basket, or box

**Directions:**

1. Cut out each child's photograph and tape it to a craft stick.

2. Print each child's name with a marker on his or her stick.

3. Store the puppets in a can, basket, or box.

4. Pull out one puppet at a time and hold it up as you sing "I Have a Friend," sung to the tune of "Farmer in the Dell."

   > I have a friend for you.
   > I have a friend for you.
   > His/her name is (<u>say child's name</u>).
   > Please be a friend, too.

**Variations:**

- Use puppets to sing this "Good Morning to You" song, sung to the tune of "Happy Birthday."

  > Good morning to you.
  > Good morning to you.
  > Good morning dear (say child's name).
  > We're glad to see you.

- When children have a disagreement, have them get each other's puppets and see if they can solve the problem. You can also use puppets to role-play classroom situations, such as name calling or hitting.

- Place puppets in a puppet theater or the classroom library.

- Photocopy children's pictures so they can make their own stick puppets of their friends.

- Glue children's photographs to toilet paper rolls to make stand-up puppets.

# PASS IT ON

Children will feel accepted and appreciated by all the positive comments from their classmates. This activity will also help them focus on each other's positive qualities.

**You will need:**

paper for each child
pens or pencils
envelope for each child

**Directions:**

Tony
friendly
nice
funny
shares
helps
good artist
awesome

1. Have each child write his or her name at the top of a sheet of paper.

2. Collect all the papers and randomly pass one out to each child. Tell them to write one positive comment about the person at the top of the paper.

3. Continue passing the papers around the room as the children write something special about each classmate. (When children get their own papers, tell them to write something they like about themselves.)

4. Collect the papers and put them in individual envelopes with their names on the front.

5. Deliver these to the children to read at the end of the day or week. Reflect on how they felt when they read what their friends said about them.

**Variations:**

✏ Use this project for an activity at the end of the school year.

✏ Arrange chairs or desks in a circle for this project.

# PEOPLE PUZZLERS

Children will be challenged by making their own puzzles, and by "putting their friends together."

**You will need:**

heavy paper or tagboard for each child

crayons

scissors

envelope for each child

shoebox

**Directions:**

1. On one side of the paper ask the children to draw a picture of themselves. Encourage them to color in the entire page.

2. Demonstrate how to turn the paper over and draw puzzle shapes. (Four to ten pieces usually work well.) Have the children cut along the lines, then put the pieces in an envelope with their name on it.

3. Store the envelopes in a shoebox and make them available to the children for independent play.

Rhonda

**Variation:**

✏ Ask older children to write a personal characteristic on the back of each piece of their puzzle. They might write their age, hobbies, special qualities, etc.

# ME BLOCKS

Won't children feel special when they decorate a block with their picture on it to add to the block center!

**You will need:**    two cardboard milk cartons (washed and dried for each child)

photos of the children

construction paper scraps

markers or crayons

glue

scissors

clear packaging tape or clear self-stick vinyl

**Directions:**

1. Cut the tops off two milk cartons. (They should each be about 4" tall.) Squeeze the sides of one so it will fit inside the other to make a block. (Make a block for each child.)

2. Cut the child's photograph to fit on one side of the block and glue it in place.

3. Cover the remaining sides of the block and the top and bottom with construction paper.

4. Let the children decorate their blocks with their name and pictures.

5. Cover the blocks with clear packaging tape or self-stick vinyl. Place in the block center.

**Variations:**

✏ Make "people blocks" by cutting different kinds of people from magazines and gluing them to milk carton blocks.

✏ Use blocks for songs, story starters, math activities, etc.

✏ Give the children their blocks to take home at the end of the school year.

# PICTURE PERFECT

**Displaying children's photographs makes them feel special and enhances their sense of self. Photographs can also be used for many learning activities in the classroom.**

*You will need:* Photos of the children (make several photocopies of each child's picture to use in the projects below)

paper

glue

scissors

crayons and markers

materials for each particular project

*Directions:*

1. Use photos of the children for identifying their cubbies or other personal belongings.

2. Glue each child's photo to the top of a file folder and write his or her name. Place all the file folders in a box or plastic crate. As children complete pictures or their work, they can file them in their folder.

3. Glue photos to construction paper. Write a sentence about some special quality each child has under his or her picture. Put the pages together to make a book.

4. Put a piece of Velcro® (loop side) on the back of each photo to use on the flannel board. To dismiss children to line up or go to an activity, place their picture on the flannel board.

5. Make two copies of each photo. Cut paper into 3-inch squares and glue the photos to the paper. Mix up the photos; then let the children match those that are alike. A memory game can also be played by having children turn photos over to try to match like pairs.

6. Put copies of photos in the Writing Center. Let children write letters to their friends in the class, then glue their friend's photo on the front of the envelope.

7. Use photos for grouping, counting, making sets, number stories, and other math activities.

*Variation:* ✏ It's equally important to display photographs of children's families in your classroom.

# "THE BEST THING ABOUT ME" TV

This "TV show" is one all of the children will agree on. Feelings of self-worth, as well as a sense of community, will be nurtured with this project.

**You will need:**
cardboard box (copier paper box works well)
utility knife*
markers or crayons
two wooden dowels cut six inches longer than the box
butcher paper
tape

**Directions:**

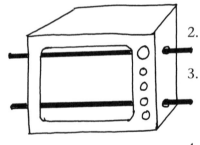

1. To make the television screen, cut an opening out of the bottom of the box.

2. Cut two holes opposite each other in the sides of the box in which to insert the wooden dowels.

3. Tear off a piece of butcher paper 15 feet to 20 feet long. (Each child in the room will need approximately 12 inches on which to draw a picture.) Trim the sides of the butcher paper so it is slightly shorter than the length of the box.

4. Talk about special characteristics of each child. Ask them to pick the best thing about themselves and illustrate it on the butcher paper. (Make sure children write their names by their illustrations.)

5. Tape the end of the butcher paper to the top wooden dowel.

6. Roll up the paper strip around the top dowel.

7. Tape the other end of the paper to the bottom dowel.

8. Slowly turn the bottom dowel to reveal the "best thing" about each child.

**Variations:**
✏ Create a title for the beginning of the show and credits for the end.
✏ Let children make a tape recording to accompany the "TV show."
✏ Have older children write a sentence to go along with their pictures.

**Hint:**
*Be sure the children do not use the utility knife.

# "I CAN DO SOMETHING SPECIAL" DAY

Children love celebrations, so this will be a fun way to let them perform and show their special talents.

***You will need:***     no materials are needed

***Directions:***

1. On Monday begin a discussion about how we all have special talents. Encourage the children to tell the different things that they can do well.

2. Ask them if they would like to have an "I Can Do Something Special" Day at the end of the week. Everyone who wants to may sing a song, tell a joke, share their art work, tell a story, do a gymnastic stunt, or do a trick.

3. Remind the children daily about the "I Can Do Something Special" Day.

4. On Friday, let the children get up one at a time and share their special talent. Remind them ahead of time about applauding for their friends and being considerate of others' feelings. (Do not force children to participate, but do encourage them.)

***Variations:***

✎ Make a video of the children. Play it back for them to watch or let them take it home to watch it with their families.

✎ Involve children in preparing a special snack to enjoy after their performance.

✎ Let children divide into small groups and sing songs, do skits, or share other talents.

# PICTURE PORTFOLIOS

**Children's self-portraits reflect how they feel about themselves and "tell a story" about their development as they grow and change.**

*You will need:*   paper
crayons, makers, paints (body colors)
construction paper
mirror

*Directions:*

1. At the beginning of the school year, ask the children to draw pictures of themselves. (Provide them with a mirror so they can "see" what they look like.) Date the pictures and let the children dictate or write a sentence to go along with them. Save and file in each child's folder.

2. Each month ask the children to draw another picture of themselves. Date the pictures and have the children write or dictate sentences before filing.

3. At the end of the year, put the pictures together to make a book to send home with the children. Let the children decorate the covers of their book.

*Variations:*

✐ Lay out the pictures for parents at your end-of-year conference. How have the drawings changed? Can they see their child's growth from the pictures?

✐ Choose a different theme each month for the pictures. You might ask the children to draw their family, school, friends, a class field trip, a party, etc.

# MYSTERY FRIEND

Children will enjoy being "detectives" as they solve who the mystery friend is. This activity also enhances reading skills.

**You will need:**

chart paper
markers
crayons

**Directions:**

Mystery Friend
1. My eyes are brown.
2. My hair is black.
3. I like to paint.
4. I can swim.
5. My pet is a cat.
Who am I?

1. Gather the children together and explain that you will need their help to identify the mystery person you are going to describe.

2. Write "mystery friend" at the top of the chart. (Think of a child who will be the mystery friend, but don't tell the children!)

3. Write the following clue on the chart:

   "My eyes are (<u>eye color of the mystery friend.</u>)."

   Ask the children to read the sentence with you. Can they tell who it is yet?

4. Write the second clue:

   "My hair is (<u>hair color of the mystery friend</u>)."

   Have the children read that clue and try to guess who it is.

5. Continue writing clues on the chart. You can use physical descriptions, likes, or other information unique to that child.

6. Have the children read all the clues together, then ask the mystery friend to please stand up.

7. Let the mystery friend draw his or her picture on the chart. Hang it in the classroom, then roll it up and send it home with the mystery friend.

**Variation:**

✏ Older children can write their own personal descriptions. Read them to the class as the children try to identify who it is.

# ALL KINDS OF SMART

Children's individual talents and abilities will be highlighted with this project.

***You will need:***

chart paper
markers and crayons
construction paper
stapler

***Directions:***

1. Ask the children what it means to be "smart." Have them brainstorm all the different ways people can be smart. (Consider music, writing, athletics, art, problem-solving, making friends, etc.)

2. Write the talents and other ways children suggest they can be "smart" on the chart paper.

3. Read the list. Then have each child choose one or two words from the chart that describe themselves.

4. Ask each child to draw a picture of themselves that shows how they are "smart." Have them write or dictate a sentence to go with the picture.

5. Staple the pictures together to make a book called "All Kinds of Smart."

***Variation:***

✏ Let children pantomime their talents as classmates try to guess what they are.

# WONDERFUL WORDS PLACEMAT

Children will enjoy creating their personal placemat and the "wonderful words" will remind them how special they are.

**You will need:**

one sheet of 12" × 18" construction paper for each child

laminating machine or clear self-stick vinyl

crayons or markers

scissors

**Directions:**

1. Give each child a sheet of construction paper. (Let them cut scallops or other designs around the outside if they wish.)

2. Have the children write their name in the middle of the paper and draw a picture of themselves.

3. Ask the children to think of "wonderful words" that describe themselves. What are some nice things other people say about them? Let the children write the words on their placemat, or have an adult write the words children dictate to them.

4. Laminate the placemats or cover them with clear self-stick vinyl.

5. Choose helpers to put out the placemats on the table for snack or lunch. The children can find their name and sit at the place.

**Variation:**

✎ Children can also make individual "sit upons" for circle time. Cut two 12-inch circles from paper grocery sacks. Have the children decorate the circles with their name and words, then hole punch around the edges. Sew three-fourths of the way around with yarn, stuff with newspaper strips or polyfil, then sew up the remaining section.

# RADIO HOUR

In addition to listening and speaking skills, children's sense of self and their confidence will be fostered when speaking into the tape recorder.

***You will need:***
tape recorder and blank tape
toilet paper roll
aluminum foil
black tissue paper
glue

***Directions:***

1. Make a play microphone before you begin this activity by wrapping the toilet paper roll in aluminum foil. Form a ball with the tissue paper and glue it on one end of the cardboard roll.

2. Have the children sit in a circle with the tape recorder in the middle. Explain that they can help you make a radio show by talking into the tape recorder.

3. Show the children the microphone and tell them that only the person holding it may talk.

4. Turn the tape recorder on. Let the children take turns holding the microphone as they talk. You might ask them to say their name, age, something special about themselves, what they like about school, etc.

5. Play the "radio hour" later on in the day and see if the children can recognize each other's voices.

***Variations:***
&#x270F; Put the tape in the Listening Center.

&#x270F; Let children take turns taking the tape home to play for their families.

***Hint:***
Children should not be forced to participate, but if you repeat this activity several times they should feel more comfortable about doing so.

# ME BOX

This idea will spark interest from classmates about individual children in your room. Children and parents will also be excited about the special attention they receive from the activity.

**You will need:**

empty detergent box with a handle
gold or silver spray paint
glitter
glue

**Directions:**

1. Spray paint the box gold or silver.
2. Write "ME" on the front of the box with glue, then sprinkle with glitter.
3. Write a note similar to the one below and tape it to the lid of the box.

> Dear Parents,
>
> Your child is bringing home the "ME" box today. Please help him/her find special objects, photographs, souvenirs, or memorabilia to put in the box. Your child will have the opportunity to share these things with classmates tomorrow, then we will return them to you.
>
> Thanks for helping us "celebrate" your child!
>
> Sincerely,

4. Choose one child each day to take the box home, then let him or her share the special treasures at circle time the following day. (Be sure to place the objects safely in another bag so they get back home!)

**Variations:**

- Decorate a basket or cloth bag to use instead of the box.
- Have a shelf or table where children can display their objects from the "ME" box.

**Hint:**

Supervise glitter carefully with young children or substitute with glitter pens.

# VIP FOR THE WEEK

Every child's self-esteem will soar when he or she is recognized as the "Very Important Person" for the week.

**You will need:**

photos of the children
posterboard
tape
markers

**Directions:**

1. Choose one child each week to be the VIP. (Explain to the other children that they will each get a turn before the end of the year.)

2. Send a note to the parents several days ahead asking them to share photos of the child, photos of family celebrations, pets, vacations, and so forth.

3. On the posterboard write the child's name at the top as VIP for the week. Tape the photos to the board, then write what the child dictates about each picture.

4. At group time, let the VIP explain his or her poster to classmates. Encourage the other children to ask the VIP questions about the photos or other things they might want to know about them.

5. Display the poster on a bulletin board or door.

**Variations:**

- Let parents and children decorate the poster together at home, or let older children make their own posters.

- Make a language experience story about the VIP. Glue their photo to a large sheet of paper, then let the other children dictate what they like best about that person.

# WE ARE FAMILY

Children will develop language skills and family pride as they tell others about their family.

**You will need:** family photos

**Directions:**

1. Several days before doing this activity, ask each child to bring in a picture of their family. (Write a note home to parents if necessary.)

2. Have the children sit in a circle on the floor. One at a time let each child show the photo of their family. Encourage them to talk about the people in their family and how they have fun together.

3. To conclude, ask children, "What is a family? How are families alike? How are they different?"

4. Hang the photos on a bulletin board with the title "WE ARE FAMILY."

**Variations:**

✏ Ask children to draw pictures of their families to hang next to the photos.

✏ Make a book of family photos to place in your classroom library.

✏ Share family photos at the beginning of the year to help children become acquainted and to help connect the home with the school.

# VIP FAMILY

**Children will realize what a Very Important Person they are as they recognize their family members who love them.**

**You will need:**
copy of "VIP Book" (sample on next page) for each child
scissors
crayons, pencils

**Directions:**

1. Fold the paper in half, then fold in fourths and eighths as shown.

2. Open up the paper so it is just folded in half. Cut down the middle halfway on the dotted lines.

3. Open and fold in half lengthwise. Hold the ends and push in the sides to make a +.

4. Bend the pages around to make a book.

5. Talk about what a "VIP" is. Ask the children to tell you some ways their family makes them feel like a "VIP."

6. Read the pages in their book, encouraging the children to comment on the different family members who do those things for them.

7. Let the children draw pictures and fill in the blanks on each page. (Younger children can dictate their responses.)

**Variation:**

✏ Ask each child to draw a picture of something special he or she likes to do with his or her family. Put the pages together to make a class book called "Family Fun."

_____ helps me.

fold

_____ plays _____ games with me.

_____ loves me!

cut

_____ cooks me _____ good food to eat.

fold

I love my family, too.

_____ reads me _____ stories.

cut

fold

_____ tucks me _____ in bed at night.

My
V I P
Family

# NAME ART

...name are very important to them and should be used frequently when ...king to them. Their names can also be used in these art projects.

**You will need:**
glitter, beans, yarn, other collage materials
paper, cardboard, or wood scraps
crayons, paint, chalk
glue, scissors
magazines or newspapers

**Directions:**

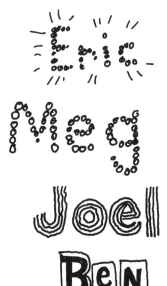

1. Let the children take turns saying their full name. Do they know where their name came from or who they were named after? Ask them to share their nicknames.

2. Choose one of the art projects below in which the children can use their names:

   *Glitter Name* — Have the children write their name in glue, then sprinkle it with glitter.

   *Texture Name* — Let the children write their name in glue, then outline it with beans, yarn, cotton, or other collage materials.

   *Ranbow Name* — Ask the children to write their name in crayon. Next, show them how to trace around their name with different colors to create a rainbow.

   *Wood Plaques* — Let the children paint their names on wood scraps.

   *Letter Collage* — Give children old magazines and newspapers and let them cut out the letters in their name and glue them on paper.

**Variations:**

✏ Obtain a library book on names to find out the meaning of each child's name.

✏ Put a large piece of paper on the classroom door for children to "sign-in" as they arrive at school each day.

**Hint:**
Supervise glitter carefully with young children or substitute with glitter pens.

# CHALK TALK

**Children can develop small motor skills as they express their individuality with "chalk talk."**

**You will need:**

colored sidewalk chalk

cement sidewalk, parking lot, or driveway

**Directions:**

1. Take children outside and give each of them a piece of chalk. (Tell them they may share with each other if they want a different color.)

2. Ask the children to draw giant pictures of themselves with the chalk. (Have them label their pictures with their names.)

3. Take a walk and admire each other's drawings.

**Variations:**

- Have the children decorate the sidewalk for each other's birthdays, holidays, or other celebrations.

- Let children trace around each other's shadows on a sunny day with chalk.

- Make your own giant sidewalk chalk. Fill a paper cup 2/3 full with plaster of paris. Add 2 teaspoons dry tempera and mix well. Stir in water to make a thick mixture. Dry several hours, then peel away the cup.

**Hints:**

- Block off an area of the parking lot on which children can play with chalk and supervise carefully.

- Be sure to get your principal's approval before doing any of these chalk projects.

# NAME POEMS

Children will focus on their special characteristics. Writing skills will be developed as they create name poems.

**You will need:**

paper
pencils

**Directions:**

Michael
Musical
interesting
curious
happy
awesome
energetic
lovable
Sancos

1. Ask the children to write their first name at the top of a sheet of paper.

2. Next, write the letters in their first name down the left-hand side.

3. Then have them write their last name at the bottom.

4. Tell the children to think of a word that describes them or something they like to do for each letter in their name.

5. Read the poem beginning with their first name and ending with their last.

**Variations:**

- Let the children illustrate their poems with crayons or markers and display them in the classroom or make a class book with them.

- You can write name poems for younger children.

- Provide children with dictionaries to help them find words for the letters in their names.

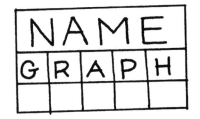

# NAME GRAPH

Children will see how special their name is as beginning sounds and language skills are reinforced.

**You will need:**

paper for each child
crayons or markers
scissors
glue
old magazines

**Directions:**

1. Have each child write his or her name across the top of the paper as shown. Evenly space the letters across the whole page. (Children with long names may wan to use a nickname.)

2. Draw vertical lines between the letters.

3. Review the letters in their names and the sounds they make. Have children think of things they like or words that describe themselves that begin with each letter.

4. Give children the magazines and ask them to cut out pictures of things they like and glue them under each letter. They may also draw pictures.

5. Allow children to share their name graphs with classmates or hang in the hallway.

**Variations:**

✎ Older children can write adjectives that describe themselves under each letter.

✎ Simplify the project for younger children by just using their initials.

✎ Have groups of children try to form friendship graphs using their names like a crossword puzzle.

```
                    E
            SHUNDRA
                E       I
         MIA        N

            NICHOLAS
                    A
                    U
                    R
            FRANKIE
```

31

# MY SPACE

Children's individuality will be recognized with their own space for displaying their work.

**You will need:**

spring-type clothespins
clothesline
markers
clear sheet protectors
clear packaging tape
bulletin board border
pushpins

**Directions:**

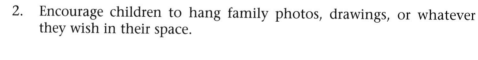

1. Create a space for each child using one of the ideas below:

   *Clothesline* — Let each child decorate his or her own clothespin with markers. Nail ends of a clothesline to a wall. Allow the children to hang their artwork, writing projects, or other things they've made with their clothespin.

   *Sheet Protectors* — Label a sheet protector with each child's name using a permanent marker. Tape the sheets to a cabinet or wall with clear tape. Children can slide their pictures or papers in the protectors as they please.

   *Mini Bulletin Boards* — Use bulletin-board borders to create a small space for each child on a wall or cork board. Label spaces with children's names, then allow children to decorate their own sections.

2. Encourage children to hang family photos, drawings, or whatever they wish in their space.

# INITIAL IT

Initials are symbols that are unique to each child. Motor and creative skills can also be developed as children do projects with their initials.

*You will need:*

posterboard
construction paper scraps
scissors, glue, tape
markers or crayons
string
hole punch
letter stencils
yarn, plastic needles, burlap

*Directions:*

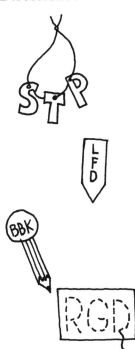

1. Print your initials on the board. Ask the children if they know what they are. Explain that each letter represents the first letter in your first, middle, and last names.

2. Help each child identify his or her initials.

3. Give them the opportunity to do one of the projects below with their initials:

   *Letter Necklace* — Have the children trace around their initials on construction paper with the letter stencils and cut them out. Punch a hole in each letter, then string it on yarn to make a necklace.

   *Bookmark* — Cut 6″ × 2-1/2″ strips of posterboard. Trim one end to a point, then let the children decorate the bookmarks with their initials.

   *Pencil Topper* — Cut 2-inch circles from construction paper scraps. Have the children write their initials on the circles, then tape them to the end of a pencil.

   *Stichery* — Let the children stitch their initials on burlap squares with yarn and plastic needles.

*Variation:*

✏ Do these projects using children's full names.

# ID BRACELET

This project focuses attention on children's names or their initials.

**You will need:**
Cardboard rollers (from toilet paper or paper towels)
dry alphabet pasta
rubbing alcohol
food coloring
plastic baggies
paper plates
glue

**Directions:**

1. Dye the pasta by separating it into four plastic baggies. Add one tablespoon of rubbing alcohol and a big squire of food coloring to each baggie. Shake. Spread on a paper plate to dry.

2. Cut the cardboard rollers into 1-1/2-inch sections. Cut a slit in the back so it will fit around the wrist.

3. Have the children select the letters in their name or their initials from the pasta and glue them onto the cardboard roller.

**Variations:**

- Let the children make words or a collage with the alphabet pasta.

- Children can decorate these cardboard bracelets with crayons or stickers and exchange them with their friends. They can also be covered with aluminum foil.

- Have the children glue the letters to a spring-type clothespin and attach a strip of magnet to the back. This can be used at home on the refrigerator to hang the children's work.

**Hint:** Be sure the children stay away from the rubbing alcohol.

# MY NAME IS

This is a fun way to learn children's names while recognizing their uniqueness. It also develops memory and motor skills.

**You will need:**  no materials are needed

**Directions:**

1. Have the children stand in a circle.

2. Ask each child to think of a motion, movement, or sound that represents him or her. (Give examples such as jumping, whistling, dancing, barking, or flapping arms like a bird.)

3. One child begins this game by saying:

   "My name is (<u>says name</u>),
   and I go (<u>does movement</u>)."

4. The second child says:

   "My name is (<u>says name</u>)
   and I go (<u>does a different movement</u>).
   His/her name is (<u>says first child's name</u>),
   and he/she goes (<u>does first child's movement</u>)."

5. The game continues with each child saying his or her name and adding a new movement before repeating what previous friends have said. (If someone forgets, classmates may help prompt him or her.)

**Variation:**  ✏ Have children act out different animals or do different exercises when it is their turn.

# TAKE A LOOK AT ME

Children will be motivated to write about themselves in these books after they've had the fun of constructing them.

**You will need:**

one sheet of 6″ × 18″ construction paper for each child
construction paper cut in 18″ × 1-1/2″ strips
small paper plates or paper cut in 6″ circles
scissors
glue
crayons, markers, writing pencils
writing paper
brad fasteners

**Directions:**

1. Have the children follow along as you demonstrate how to make the body book.

   a. Fold the sheet of construction paper in half, then fourths.

   b. Bring in the two edges to the middle to make a door.

   c. Open the door and glue a sheet of writing paper in the middle. (This will be the "body" of the book.)

   d. Take four strips of paper and bend them back and forth to make a fan. Attach the strips with brad fasteners to make arms and legs.

   e. Staple the paper plate (or paper circle) to the top to make the head.

   f. Color the head and cut out hands, feet, and other details.

2. Ask the children to think of a special story about themselves and write it in their books. (Adults can do this for younger children.)

3. Let the children share their books with classmates or tie a string to the heads and hang them in the room.

**Variation:**

✏ Use "body books" to write about favorite book characters or famous citizens.

# INVISIBLE WRITING

"Invisible" writing is a great incentive for reading and writing. The positive thoughts will also contribute to the children's self-worth.

***You will need:***

one sheet of white paper for each child
white crayon
diluted tempera paint
paintbrush

***Directions:***

1. Write a "secret" message for each child in your classroom with the white crayon on a sheet of paper. Use encouraging statements such as, "Philip is a good helper" or "Shanti has a beautiful smile." (Put their name on the back with a pencil to identify to whom each note belongs.)

2. Let each child paint over his or her secret message with the paintbrush. (The paint will resist the wax crayon and reveal the message.)

3. Give children the opportunity to share their secret messages with classmates.

***Variations:***

✏ Let children write their own invisible messages to friends and family members.

✏ Invisible writing can also be done with watercolors.

# YOU'RE WONDERFUL!

**Children will feel special as their friends sing this song to them.**

*You will need:*     no materials are needed

*Directions:*
1. Have the children sit in a circle. Choose one child to stand in the middle as you sing this song to the tune of "Dry Bones."

    We all think you're wonderful, we do.

    We give a lot of credit to you.

    We all think that (child's name) is true blue.

    We shout our praises to you, we do.

2. Let classmates tell the child in the middle what they like about him or her.

3. Continue having children stand in the middle as you sing to them and compliment them.

*Variations:*

Sarah
friendly
helpful
hard worker
good singer

- ✏ Start each morning by singing the above song to a different child. Let that child be line leader or special helper for the day.

- ✏ Write the positive comments the children say about each other on a chart tablet.

# SECRET PAL MAILBOX

The Secret Pal Mailbox is another way to encourage children and to contribute to their self-esteem.

***You will need:***

empty cereal box
sheets of red and blue paper
brad fastener
scissors
glue
writing paper
pencil

***Directions:***

1. Cut the top off the cereal box. Cover it with blue paper.

2. Cut a small flag from the red paper and attach it to the box with the brad fastener.

3. At circle time, show the children the mailbox and tell them that a "secret pal" will be watching them and will write a note to them when they do something special or kind.

4. Write a note to each child about something he or she does well and sign it "SP." Put the notes in the mailbox when the children are not looking.

5. Before the children leave at the end of the day, pretend to check the mailbox. Then deliver the notes to the children.

6. Use the box daily to send personal notes of encouragement to different children.

***Variation:***

✏ Let the children write notes to each other and place them in the mailbox.

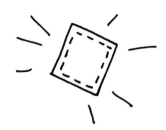

# TOSS AND TELL

This is a good activity to start the day, end the day, or to use as a transition game.

**You will need:**  beanbag or sponge ball

**Directions:**

1. Have the children sit or stand in a circle. Explain that whomever is holding the beanbag should say his or her name and something he or she can do well.

2. The first player then tosses the beanbag to a friend who catches it and tells something he or she does well.

3. The game continues with each child telling something he or she can do well.

**Variations:**

✏ Have children say something they like about a friend as they toss the beanbag to that person.

✏ Have children name favorite foods, songs, books, or other likes as they catch the beanbag.

✏ To end the school day, ask children to say one new thing they learned or enjoyed at school when they catch the beanbag.

**Hint:**  A simple beanbag can be made from an old sock, dried beans, and a rubber band. Place about a cup of dried beans in the toe of the sock. Wrap the rubber band around the beans. Pull the cuff of the sock over the beans to make a bean bag.

# NAME RAP

What a "cool" way to use language and enhance self-esteem!

**You will need:** no materials are needed

**Directions:**

1. Ask the children if they know what a "rap" is. Explain that it's like a rhyme or chant that has a strong beat.

2. Demonstrate how to clap, snap fingers, or make a "sh-sh-sh-sh" sound as you say the "Name Rap" below.

> My name is (say child's name),
> I'm proud to say.
> I'm (say age) years old,
> And I feel great today.
> I'm pretty special
> There's no one like me.
> I'll just be myself.
> That's the best way to be!

3. Use each child's name in the rap.

**Variations:**

- Encourage the children to make up their own raps about themselves.

- Make a tape of children doing their name raps.

- Let children work together in small groups to create raps about their class or school.

# BIBBITY BOBBITY BUMBLEBEE

This chant reinforces children's names and is another great game for transition times.

**You will need:**    no materials are needed

**Directions:**
1.  Children may sit on the floor or in chairs.

2.  Begin patting your thighs until the children join along. Then start the chant below using one child's name.

> Bibbity bobbity bumblebee,
> Who can say their name for me? (*Point to a child.*)
> (Say child's name.)
> (Class repeats child's name.)
> Whisper it.
> (Whisper child's name.)
> Clap it.
> (Say child's name clapping each syllable.)
> No sound.
> (Mouth child's name.)

3.  Continue saying the chant with other children's names in the class.

**Variations:**

✏ Here's another chant with children's names:

> Who ate the cookie in the cookie jar?
> (Child's name) ate the cookie in the cookie jar.
> Who me? (Child says.)
> Yes you. (Class responds.)
> Couldn't be. (Child says.)
> Then who? (Class responds.)
> (Second child's name.) (First child names a second child.)

✏ Clap or snap to this chant as you continue using different children's names.

# NAME SONGS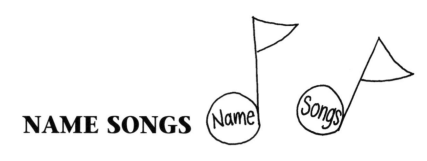

Singing lightens spirits and creates a sense of community. The songs below also use children's names and contribute to their positive feelings of self.

**You will need:**   no materials are needed

**Directions:**

1. Use this song to start your day:

   **"Here I Am"** (*Tune: "Frère Jacques"*)

   Where is (child's name)?
   Where is (child's name)?
   Here I am. (*Child sings.*)
   Here I am. (*Child sings.*)
   How are you today, (child's name)?
   Very well, I thank you. (*Child responds.*)
   Glad you're here.
   Glad you're here.

2. Sing this song while waiting:

   **"Jolly Good Friend"** (*Tune:* "Jolly Good Fellow")

   (Child's name) is a jolly good friend.
   (Child's name) is a jolly good friend.
   (Child's name) is a jolly good friend.
   And I am a good friend, too.

3. Give children a hug when you sing this tune:

   **"Little Red Box"** (*Tune:* **"Polly Wolly Doodle"**)

   I wish I had a little red box
       to put my (child's name) in.
   I'd take him/her out and go
       Hug, hug, hug.
   And put him/her back again.

4. Release wiggles with this chant:

   (Child's name), (Child's name),
   Sick in bed. Called the doctor
   and the doctor said,
   "Get up, (child's name). You're not sick.
   All you need is an exercise trick."
   So stand up and shakey, shakey, shakey.   (*Child
   Get down and shakey, shakey, shakey.    stands up
   Turn around and shakey, shakey, shakey.   and shakes
   Sit down and shakey, shakey, shakey.    to the chant.*)

# I AM SPECIAL

Here's a song to help children focus on their unique qualities.

**You will need:**     empty photo frame or posterboard cut in a 9" × 12" frame

**Directions:**
1. Have the children sit on the floor in a circle.

2. Sing the first verse of this song as you look through the picture frame:

   **"I Am Special"** (*Tune:* "Frère Jacques")

   I am special,
   I am special.
   Take a look.
   You will see.
   Someone very special,
   Someone very special.
   And it's me! (*Point to self.*)
   And it's me!

3. Say something that you like about yourself, then pass the frame to a child. Ask the child to look through the frame as you sing the song to him or her.

4. Have the child say what's special about himself or herself, or ask class-mates to tell what they like about him or her.

5. Continue passing the frame and singing to each child.

**Variation:**
✏ Use the picture frame to sing this song:

   **"I'm Looking Through My Window"**
   (*Tune:* "Go In and Out My Window")

   I'm looking through my window.     (*Look through*
   I'm looking through my window.     *frame.*)
   I'm looking through my window,
   and I see my friend (child's name).

Children take turns looking through the "window" as you sing to them. They may then pass the "window" to a friend.

# ALL BY MYSELF

This tune will encourage children to be independent and will entertain them during routine transitions.

**You will need:**   no materials are needed

**Directions:**

1. As children clean up or get dressed, sing this song to the tune of "Flies in the Buttermilk."

   > I can put on my coat
   > All by myself.
   > I can put on my coat
   > All by myself.
   > I can put on my coat
   > All by myself.
   > How about you, my darling?

2. Find one child doing what you asked and sing his or her name in the song.

3. Continue using children's names in the song as they join along.

**Variations:**

- ✐ Change the words for whatever behavior you are encouraging, such as "I can pick up the toys" or "I can wash my hands."

- ✐ Let the children draw pictures of things they can do all by themselves. Put the pages together to make a class book called "All by Myself."

- ✐ Here's another song to sing to children to encourage independence:

   **"I Am Independent"** (*Tune:* "Frère Jacques")

   > I am independent.
   > I am independent.
   > I can do it myself.
   > I can do it myself.
   > If I cannot do it.
   > If I cannot do it.
   > I will ask for help.
   > I will ask for help.

# BROWNIE BEAR STORY

This story reinforces the concept that you like the children just the way they are and they should always try to be themselves.

**You will need:**

file folder

8″ × 10″ sheets of brown, red, yellow, green, blue, and brown construction paper

tape

scissors

bear pattern

**Directions:**

1. On one side of the file folder cut out a bear using the pattern on the following page.

2. Tape the sides of the file folder together.

3. Insert the construction paper into the file folder in this order: brown, red, yellow, green, blue, brown.

4. Begin telling the story below. Encourage the children to join you in the chorus.

   Once there was a little bear named Brownie Bear. He was not happy because he always wanted to change colors and be something that he was not.

   One day he went walking and he saw some juicy, red strawberries. "Oh, what fun to be red," he thought as he said:

(*Chorus*)   I'm Brownie the Bear
as you can see,
and I can change colors,
one, two, three!          (*Say slowly as you
clap your hands.*)

# BROWNIE BEAR STORY
## *(Continued)*

And he turned red! (*Remove the brown sheet of paper in front to make the bear red.*) What a silly bear!

Brownie Bear walked along until he came to a yellow duck and he said:

(*Chorus*)      I'm Brownie the Bear
as you can see,
and I can change colors,
one, two, three!

And he turned yellow! (*Remove the red sheet of paper in front to make the bear yellow.*) What a silly bear!

Brownie walked on until he came to a green turtle, and he said:

      (*Repeat the chorus.*)

And he turned green! (*Remove the yellow paper.*) What a silly bear!

Brownie walked along until he came to a blue bird, and he said:

      (*Repeat the chorus.*)

And he turned blue! (*Remove the green paper.*) What a silly bear!

Brownie was getting hungry, so he decided to go home. But when he got there his mother didn't recognize him because he was blue, so he said:

      (*Repeat the chorus.*)

And he turned brown! (*Remove the blue paper.*) Brownie's mother said, "Oh my little brown bear. Now I know who you are. I love you just the way you are!" Then she gave him a great, big, bear hug!

5. Conclude the story by talking about why the children are special just the way they are!

# HANDS UP FOR US

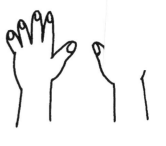

This project will help children focus on their accomplishments. It is also a way to recognize the children when they achieve a goal.

**You will need:**

construction paper
scissors
markers or crayons
tape

**Directions:**

1. Explain that there are many different things we can do to make ourselves feel proud. Have children suggest things they are proud of about themselves.

2. Give each child a sheet of construction paper. Ask them to trace around their hands and cut them out. (Remind children to work with a friend if they need help with this.)

3. Have the children write one thing they can do well or one thing they are proud of about themselves on each hand. (Younger children can draw pictures or dictate this to an adult.)

4. As children describe their accomplishment to classmates, tape their hands to a wall or bulletin board. Add the title: "Hands Up for Us."

5. Encourage the children to add additional handprints as they learn new things or accomplish new goals.

**Variation:**

✍ Do this activity at the end of the year to reflect on how much they have learned during the year.

# "ME" MOBILE

Children will feel special with their own personal mobile, and they'll have the opportunity to express their creativity.

**You will need:**
one coat hanger for each child
construction paper for each child
scissors
hole punch
yarn
markers or crayons

**Directions:**

1. Give each child a coat hanger.

2. Have them draw pictures of themselves, their families, pets, homes, friends, likes, etc., on the construction paper.

3. Let them cut out the objects and punch holes in the pictures.

4. Tie different lengths of yarn to the pictures. Then tie them on the hanger.

5. Have the children explain their mobiles to classmates. Then hang them in the room.

**Variations:**

✏ Let the children cut out the letters in their name or their initials and tie them on a hanger.

✏ Children can also cut pictures from old magazines to create a mobile about themselves.

# BODY ART

Children's self-awareness and uniqueness will be developed as they trace around their bodies and do various projects with the tracings.

**You will need:**

butcher paper
pencil
scissors
crayons, paints, or markers (body colors)
full-length mirror

**Directions:**

1. Roll out the butcher paper on the floor and let one child at a time lie down.

2. Trace around each child's body with a pencil. Then give them markers, paints, or crayons with which to decorate their bodies. (A full-length mirror will give children the opportunity to look at themselves as they work.)

3. Let the children cut out their bodies. Then hang them in the classroom or hallway.

4. Talk about how everyone's body is alike *and* how the bodies are different. Be positive.

**Variations:**

✆ Provide children with yarn, buttons, fabric, wallpaper scraps, and other collage materials to decorate their paper bodies.

✆ Have the children take home the outline of their body and decorate it with their parents to represent the dress of their ancestors.

✆ Let the children decorate their paper bodies to reflect what they want to be when they grow up.

✆ Attach the arms and legs to the children's paper bodies with brad fasteners so they can move.

✆ Make giant puzzles out of their paper bodies by having the children cut them into puzzle pieces.

✆ Have the children write words on their paper bodies that describe themselves.

# DESIGNER T-SHIRT

Children will have fun designing and wearing their own special T-shirt.

**You will need:**

old T-shirts (white works best)

paper

fabric crayons (available at craft and sewing stores)

iron and flat surface

**Directions:**

1. Several days ahead explain to the children that they will get to design their very own T-shirt. Ask them to bring in an old shirt from home, or send a note to the parents about it.

2. Give each child a piece of paper and have them draw a picture of themselves with the fabric crayons. Encourage them to draw pictures of what makes them special or something they can do well. Remind them to press firmly with the crayons. The darker the color, the better their design will show up. (If words are used, they must be written backwards.)

3. Let the children place their designs where they want them on their shirts. (Place the crayon side down.) Next, an adult will need to iron over the paper with a hot iron, pressing firmly until the design transfers onto the shirt.

**Variation:**

✏ Children will also enjoy making personalized bandannas. Cut old sheets or muslin into 24-inch squares. Then cut the squares in half diagonally to make two triangles. Let the children decorate the triangles with permanent markers and wear them around their necks.

**Hint:**

Be sure the children stay away from the hot iron.

# FIVE SENSES BOOK

Self-awareness, likes, and dislikes are explored when children construct their own book about their senses.

***You will need:***
five paper lunch bags for each child
hole punch
book ring or yarn
scissors, glue
old magazines or catalogs
crayons or markers

***Directions:***

1. Following a unit or discussion of the five senses, give each child five lunch bags.

2. On the first bag, have the children draw around their hand. Then have them cut out magazine pictures of things they like to feel. Put these in the bag.

3. On the second bag, have them draw their mouth. Then cut out things they like to eat and put these in the bag.

4. On the third bag, let them draw their eyes and then cut out things they like to see. Put these in the bag.

5. On the fourth bag, ask them to draw their nose and then cut out items they like to smell. Put these in the bag.

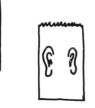

6. On the fifth bag, the children should draw their ears and then cut out noises they like to hear. Put these in the bag.

7. Punch a hole in the upper left-hand corner of each bag. Then put them together with a book ring or piece of yarn.

8. Have the children look in each other's bags and compare likes and dislikes.

***Variations:***

✎ Print a sentence on each bag, such as, "I like to smell things" or "My ears can hear."

✎ Take a listening walk and see how many different sounds the children can identify.

✎ Plan a tasting party where each child brings a healthy snack to share.

✎ Make a texture collage of different objects children can feel, such as cotton, sandpaper, corrugated cardboard, sticky tape, bubblewrap, satin, etc.

# SILHOUETTES

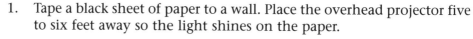

**Individual differences and self-acceptance will be explored with this silhouette project.**

**You will need:** overhead projector or other bright light source
sheets of black and white paper
pencils
tape
scissors
glue
chair

**Directions:**

1. Tape a black sheet of paper to a wall. Place the overhead projector five to six feet away so the light shines on the paper.

2. Have one child at a time sit on a chair sideways between the light and paper so his or her shadow can be seen on the paper. Trace around the shadow with a pencil.

3. Cut out the silhouette or let the child cut it out and glue it to the white paper.

4. Hold up the silhouettes one at a time and see if the children can identify who they belong to.

5. Display the silhouettes on a bulletin board or in the hallway.

**Variations:**

- Parents always appreciate receiving their child's silhouette as a gift.

- Make silhouettes on white paper, then offer children body-color paints to paint them.

- Let children write words or draw pictures that describe themselves on their silhouettes.

# MY BACKPACK

Children will have the opportunity to use creative skills as they make their own unique backpack.

**You will need:**
one large empty cereal box for each child
butcher paper
thin rope or heavy twine
crayons, markers, or paints
scissors
tape
hole punch

**Directions:**

1. Several days before doing this project, ask the children to bring in empty cereal boxes.

2. Cut the tops off the boxes.

3. Let the children wrap their boxes in butcher paper, leaving the tops open.

4. Give the children crayons, markers, or paints to decorate their boxes. Encourage them to write their names and draw pictures of themselves doing things they enjoy or do well.

5. Punch four holes in the back as shown. Cut two pieces of rope or twine that are 16 to 20 inches long. Thread the rope through the holes and knot them on the inside to make shoulder straps.

**Variations:**

✏ Make a snack or picnic lunch to put in the backpack and go on a walk or hike.

✏ Children will also enjoy making "note totes" in which they can carry their work home. Let them decorate cardboard rollers from paper towels with crayons or markers. Paintings, notes, and other school work can be rolled up, slipped in the tube, and easily carried home.

# "HOORAY FOR ME" WINDSOCK

Language skills and self-appreciation will be reinforced as children make and explain their windsocks to classmates.

**You will need:**

18" × 8" construction paper or posterboard
tissue paper cut in 1" × 16" strips
crayons or markers
scissors, glue, hole punch, stapler
string or yarn cut in 12" pieces

**Directions:**

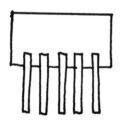

1. Give each child a piece of construction paper or posterboard.

2. Show them how to lay their paper horizontally in front of them. Then let them decorate it with their names, pictures, favorite foods, hobbies, etc.

3. Turn the paper over and glue the strips of tissue paper to the bottom edge as shown.

4. Wrap the ends around to form a cylinder and staple in place.

5. Punch three holes evenly spaced along the top edge.

6. Tie a piece of string in each hole. Then bring the ends of the strings together and knot.

7. Ask the children to share their windsocks with classmates. Then hang them in the room.

**Variations:**

- Let children decorate their windsocks with magazine pictures, photos, or other collage materials.

- Use this project at the beginning of the school year to help children get to know each other.

- Send home directions and materials for making windsocks. Then let parents help their children decorate this project.

- Use windsocks for illustrating favorite books or to culminate a unit of study.

# GOOD CENTS!

**What fun to see your face on a coin and to imagine that you are a famous person!**

***You will need:***    coins (pennies, nickels, dimes, quarters)
paper cut in 8" circles
crayons or markers

***Directions:***

1. Hold up the coins one at a time and ask the children to name them and tell the values. Talk about the different Presidents on the coins and what they contributed to our country.

2. Pass the coins around so the children can examine them closely.

3. Ask the children how they would feel if their face were on a coin.

4. Pass out the paper circles to the children and ask them to design a coin with their face on it.

5. Have the children show their coins and tell what they would do to contribute to our country.

***Variations:***

- Hang the coins on a bulletin board or punch a hole in them and hang them from the ceiling with a piece of string.

- Let the children draw their face as it might look on a dollar bill or on a stamp.

- Have children make trading cards with their pictures. Cut out cardboard the size of baseball cards. Let them draw their face on the front and then write statistics about themselves on the back.

# BANNER HANG-UPS

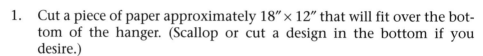

**This is a unique way for children to create and display a poster about themselves.**

***You will need:***
    one coat hanger for each child
    paper
    crayons or markers
    glue
    scissors
    old magazines

***Directions:***

1. Cut a piece of paper approximately 18″ × 12″ that will fit over the bottom of the hanger. (Scallop or cut a design in the bottom if you desire.)

2. Let the children write their names on the banners and then decorate them. Children might draw pictures of themselves, their families, pets, friends, homes, and so forth. They could also cut out magazine pictures of things they like, favorite foods, or what they want to be when they grow up.

3. Glue banners to the bottom of hangers. Have the children share them with classmates. Then hang them from the ceiling.

***Variations:***

    ✏ Use felt to make banners. Decorate the banners with glitter, felt scraps, and other sewing notions.

    ✏ Illustrate favorite books on banners or use banners to culminate a unit or theme.

***Hint:***
    Supervise glitter carefully with young children or substitute with glitter pens.

# FLAGS AND PENNANTS

Flags and pennants are other projects that focus on children's individuality and make them feel special.

**You will need:**
examples of flags and pennants
colorful construction paper
markers, crayons, and paints
scissors
glue
glitter
stapler
straws

**Directions:**

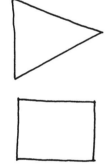

1. Cut the construction paper into flag and pennant shapes (rectangles and triangles).

2. Show the children the different examples of flags and pennants. How are colors and symbols used on the flags? What symbols would you use to design a flag or pennant to represent you?

3. Let the children choose either a flag or pennant shape and decorate it with their name, symbols, glitter, etc.

4. Staple the flags and pennants to straws. Then let the children march around the room in a parade.

**Variations:**

- Give the children a ball of clay to stick their flags in on their desks.
- Tie a piece of string across the room and staple the children's flags and pennants to it.
- Make pennants for field day or other school event.
- Use felt or fabric scraps to make flags.

**Hint:**
Supervise glitter carefully with young children or substitute with glitter pens.

# PEOPLE WHO LOVE ME

This activity will give children the opportunity to reflect on how many people really do love them.

**You will need:**
one sheet of 12″ × 18″ white paper for each child
red construction paper
crayons or markers (body colors)
scissors
glue

**Directions:**

1. Teach this poem to the children:

   I'm pretty special.
   There's no one else like me.
   And there are many people
   Who really do love me!

2. Ask the children to name some people who love them.

3. Cut out red heart and write "People who love me" on them. Give one to each child and let them glue it to their sheet of white paper.

4. Have children draw pictures of all the people who love them on their paper. Label the pictures.

5. Fold in one inch from the sides all the way around to create a frame.

6. Encourage the children to hang their pictures at home and add to them as they think of other people who love them.

**Variations:**

✐ Let children draw pictures of people who love them on paper plates. Attach a piece of yarn for hanging.

✐ Have children write letters to people they love.

# A LETTER TO MYSELF

As children write this letter to themselves, they can focus on what they are like now and set goals for themselves in the future.

**You will need:**   paper
pen or pencil
ribbon

**Directions:**

1. Ask the children to think about what they will be like when they graduate from elementary school. How old will they be? What will they look like? What kinds of activities will they be involved in?

2. Pass out paper to the children and ask them to write a letter to themselves when they graduate from elementary school. Suggest they describe what they think they will be like, their hobbies, friends, sports they'll enjoy, etc.

3. Let the children roll up their letters and tie a ribbon around them.

4. Tell the children to take their letters home and put them in a safe place. Remind them not to open them until their graduation day.

**Variations:**

✏ Collect the letters and send them to the parents with a note asking them to save them until their child graduates from elementary school.

✏ Let the children write letters to themselves when they graduate from high school or turn 21.

✏ Have the children write letters to themselves at the beginning of the school year describing what they think their year will be like, what they'll learn, etc. Return the letters the last day of school.

# "MY FAVORITE THINGS" BAG BOOK

Children will be able to share their favorite things with classmates with these bag books. Visual and motor skills will also be reinforced.

***You will need:***

4 or 5 paper lunch bags for each child

stapler

scissors

tape

old magazines or catalogs

***Directions:***

1. Pass out four or five lunch bags to each child. Staple the open ends together to make a book.

2. Fold over the bottom of each bag to make a peek-a-boo flap.

3. Let the children look through magazines and catalogs to find pictures of things they like.

4. Have them glue one picture to each bag so part of it is showing and the other part is hidden under the flap.

5. Write "My Favorite Things" on the first bag.

6. Let the children trade books with their friends and try to guess the different partial pictures. They can open the flaps to confirm their guesses.

***Variations:***

✎ Let the children draw their own pictures of their favorite things on the bags.

✎ Have the children write or dictate sentences about the pictures on the bags.

# A LITTLE BOOK ABOUT ME

Children's self-esteem will be enhanced when they make this book that highlights their special characteristics. They will also be encouraged to read and write.

**You will need:** copies of the following two pages for each child
crayons and pencils
scissors
stapler

**Directions:**
1. Give each child copies of the pages for the book.

2. Have them cut the pages apart along the dotted lines and arrange them in order. Staple.

3. Read the pages with the children. Then let them independently complete the sentences and draw small pictures. (Younger children can dictate their sentences to an adult.)

**Variations:**
✏ Do a few pages of the book at a time. Then put them together.

✏ Make a similar book for each child using 8-1/2″ × 11″ sheets of paper.

**1**

**2**

# About Me

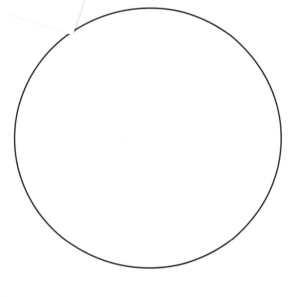

by _____

This is me.
I am _____ years old.

**3**

**4**

This is my family.

This is my home.

**5**

Here is my pet. (Or what
I would like for a pet.)

These are my friends.

**7**

**8**

I am special because _____

_____

Things I like.

_____.

# IT'S MY BIRTHDAY!

Birthdays are a wonderful time to celebrate the individual children in your room. These ideas are sure to make children feel special, and the birthday book will be a remembrance of their day.

**You will need:**
construction paper
drawing paper
crayons or markers
glitter
stickers
glue
scissors
stapler

**Directions:**

1. When preparing your monthly calendar, note children's birthdays so they can anticipate and count the days.
2. Make a banner for your door that says, "Happy Birthday to (<u>child's name</u>)."
3. Cut out a crown for the birthday child from construction paper that is approximately 24 inches long. Let the child decorate it with glitter and stickers; then size it to their head and staple.
4. Sing the traditional birthday song at group time. Sing this second verse:

   > How old are you?
   > How old are you?
   > Dear (<u>child's name</u>),
   > How old are you?

   Together clap out the number of years old the child is.
5. Give each child in the room a sheet of drawing paper and ask him or her to draw a picture for the birthday child. Meanwhile, let the birthday child decorate the construction paper to make a cover for the book.
6. Have the children individually give their pictures to the birthday child with a wish. Put the pages in the construction paper to make a book and staple.

**Variation:**

✏ Decorate the birthday child's desk or chair.

**Hints:**

✏ Be sure to celebrate the summer birthdays, too!
✏ Supervise glitter carefully with young children or substitute with glitter pens.

# BADGES AND AWARDS

Children love wearing awards and being recognized for special accomplishments. These badges will enhance their self-esteem and are a tangible way to point out their unique qualities.

***You will need:***

copies of the awards on the following two pages

markers or crayons

scissors

tape

***Directions:***

1. Make copies of the badges on the following pages. Cut the two pages apart so you can use the badges separately.

2. Pass out one of the badges to each child. Let him or her tell you what's special about himself or herself as you write his or her sentence on the badge.

3. Have the children decorate their badges with crayons or markers and cut them out.

4. Tape the badges to the children. Or punch a hole in the badges and tie on a piece of yarn to make a necklace.

***Variations:***

- Let the children decorate their awards with glitter, sequins, ribbon, and other craft supplies.

- Laminate the badges or cover them with clear self-stick vinyl so they will last longer.

- Have children design their own badges from construction paper and collage materials.

***Hint:***

Supervise glitter carefully with young children or substitute with glitter pens.

I'm Special because _____ _____ _____.

Wonderful Me I can____ _____.

I'm a star!

_____ (Name) World's Greatest _____ (Talent)

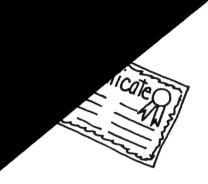

# CERTIFICATES

Children will be very proud of their "official certificate." These certificates will also give parents something positive to recognize in their children.

**You will need:**
copies of the certificates on the following page
pen
patriotic or inspirational music
wooden block or small stool

**Directions:**

1. Fill in a certificate for each child with his or her name and something special about him or her.

2. Gather the children together for an "awards ceremony."

3. Play the music. As you call out each child's name, have the child come up and stand on the platform (block or stool) as you hand him or her the certificate and shake his or her hand. Read what it says on the certificate and encourage classmates to applaud for each other.

**Variations:**

✍ Copy the certificates on colored paper and add a gold sticker or star.

✍ Use the certificates for individual recognition, such as losing a tooth, learning to write his or her name, etc.

✍ Let the children dictate what is special about themselves as you write it on their certificate.

✍ Have children decorate their own certificates with glitter, stickers, and ribbon.

**Hint:**
Supervise glitter carefully with young children or substitute with glitter pens.

# CERTIFICATE OF ACCOMPLISHMENT

Presented to _____
(Child's Name)

For _____

_____

Date _____        _____

Teacher's Signature

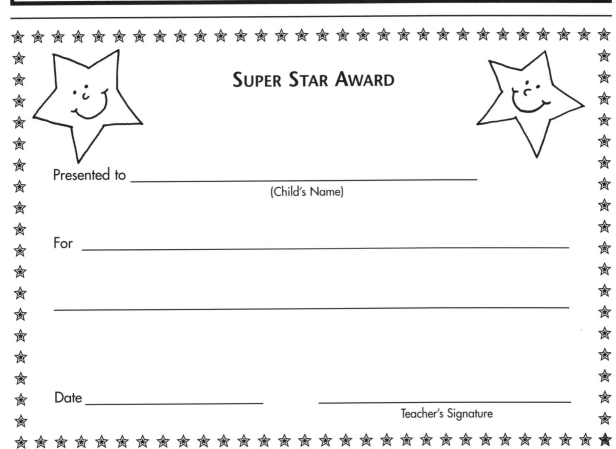

## SUPER STAR AWARD

Presented to _____
(Child's Name)

For _____

_____

Date _____        _____

Teacher's Signature

71

# 2

# Friends, Friends, Friends

Friendship and self-esteem are intricately interrelated. Children with a positive self-esteem are more attractive to their peers, and children with many friends have a higher self-esteem. The activities in this section will help children develop positive social skills, encourage them to think about what it takes to be a friend, and provide them with experiences in working cooperatively. Through these activities children will also be developing language skills, creativity, problem-solving strategies, and other curriculum goals. Above all, a sense of "community" in the classroom will be enhanced with these projects and games.

# FRIENDSHIP WEB

Creating a friendship web is a special bonding activity for children and will contribute to their language skills.

***You will need:***     a ball of yarn

***Directions:***

1. Have the children sit on the floor in a circle.

2. Hold the ball of yarn and wrap it around your hand loosely one time. Say one thing you like about one child in your room; then roll the ball of yarn to that child.

3. That child takes the ball of yarn, wraps it around his or her hand, says something nice about a friend, and then rolls the yarn to that friend.

4. The game continues until every child has had a turn. Everyone then slips the yarn from their hand and lays it on the floor, creating a "friendship web."

***Variations:***

✏ Reverse the process, winding the ball of yarn as you go backwards.

✏ Use this game to tell an original group story, to share secret feelings, to say things that make you feel proud of yourself, and so forth.

# THE CAR WASH

Children will get warm feelings from their friends that will enhance their self-worth. This activity will also give children the opportunity to focus on the positive qualities of their classmates.

*You will need:*  no materials are needed

*Directions:*

1. Divide the class into two groups.

2. Have each group stand side by side in a line facing each other. (The lines should be about two feet apart.)

3. Tell the children to pretend they are a car wash. (Demonstrate how to move your hands in a circular motion like the brushes.)

4. Choose one child at a time to be the "car" that goes through the car wash. Ask the other children to *gently* touch that person and say something they like about him or her as he or she moves slowly between the two lines.

5. Let children take turns going through the "car wash."

6. After the activity, reflect on how they felt when they went through the "car wash."

*Variation:*

✏ Do a similar activity with a "friendship machine" where children walk around the inside of a circle as fellow classmates pat them on the back and say kind things.

# FRIEND BINGO

This is a great "get acquainted" activity to start the school year, or it can be used to "renew" friendships.

**You will need:**   one copy of "Friend BINGO" for each child
pencils

**Directions:**

1. Pass out a "Friend BINGO" sheet to each child.

2. Read all of the items so children are familiar with what they are looking for.

3. When you say "GO," each child moves around the room trying to fill up his or her card by having a different friend sign his or her name or initials in each square.

4. The object of the game is to see if everyone can fill up his or her card. (You might give a prize to the first and last persons to complete their cards.)

**Variation:**   ✏ Simplify this activity for younger children by using pictures of different things they would like in the squares. Let friends color in the picture of what they like best.

# FRIEND BINGO

| | | | |
|---|---|---|---|
| has a cat<br><br>_____ | likes pizza<br><br>_____ | is a big sister<br><br>_____ | likes bugs<br>and spiders<br><br>_____ |
| plays baseball<br><br>_____ | favorite color<br>is purple<br><br>_____ | reads a lot<br><br>_____ | is a chocolate<br>lover<br><br>_____ |
| is a big brother<br><br>_____ | likes horses<br><br>_____ | has a pet bird<br><br>_____ | likes to play<br>outside<br><br>_____ |
| likes to ride<br>a bike<br><br>_____ | enjoys singing<br><br>_____ | likes to watch TV<br><br>_____ | has a computer<br><br>_____ |
| has a baby<br>brother or sister<br><br>_____ | likes to swim<br><br>_____ | listens to music<br><br>_____ | has a dog<br><br>_____ |

# FRIENDSHIP CHAIN

This is an interesting project to help children get to know each other and foster a feeling of community in the classroom.

**You will need:**
colored construction paper cut in 9″ × 2″ strips
crayons or markers
stapler

**Directions:**

1. Give each child a strip of paper. Ask the children to write their name on the strip and decorate it with crayons or markers.

2. One child at a time takes his or her strip and staples it to another strip to make a chain. As each child staples his or her strip, they describe themselves and why they would make a good friend.

3. Conclude by hanging the "friendship chain" in the classroom. Emphasize how important each individual is and what would happen if one strip broke.

**Variations:**

✏ Make friendship chains using school colors or seasonal colors.

✏ Allow each child to make his or her own friendship chain at the end of the school year. Give each child as many strips as there are students in the room. Have them write their names and phone numbers on each strip. Children exchange strips with each other, then glue them together to make a keepsake of their classmates. They can also use it to call friends when they are out of school.

# RECIPE FOR A WONDERFUL CLASS

As children focus on the positive qualities of a classroom, they will become aware of how they can contribute to the group.

**You will need:**

chart paper
markers

**Directions:**

Recipe for a
Wonderful Class
1. Friends help each other.
2. We obey the rules.
3. We try our best.
4. We work together.

1. Gather the children and tell them what a wonderful class they are. Ask them to think about what makes them so special.

2. Write "Recipe for a Wonderful Class" on the chart paper. As the children tell you what makes their class so wonderful, write down their statements on the chart.

3. Read the list together.

4. Ask the children how they can contribute to their class to make it even better.

5. Hang the chart on the wall and refer to it occasionally to renew desired behavior.

**Variations:**

✏ Use this activity at the beginning of the school year to establish goals.

✏ Give each child a recipe card and let them write out their individual recipes for a "wonderful class," "special friend," "good citizen," and so forth.

# THE FRIEND BOOK

"The Friend Book" will help children identify positive behaviors for being a friend that they should emulate. It will also point out negative behaviors they should avoid.

**You will need:**

8-1/2" × 11" paper
crayons or markers
pens or pencils
12" × 18" sheet of construction paper
hole punch
yarn

**Directions:**

1. Ask the children to describe positive qualities of friends; then ask them to suggest things that friends should not do to each other.

2. Give each child a piece of paper and demonstrate how to fold it in half. Draw a line down the fold. On the left side ask them to draw a picture of what a friend should do. On the right side have them draw a picture of what a friend should *not* do.

3. Have children dictate or write a sentence to go under each picture.

4. Put the pages between the construction paper to make a book. Hole punch at the top and tie with yarn. Write "The Friend Book" on the cover.

5. Read the book to the class, encouraging their comments and reflections.

**Variations:**

✏ Ask children to role-play things friends should and should not do.

✏ Have children describe the "perfect friend." How can they be more like the "perfect friend" they would like to have?

✏ To vary journal writing, let the children make a "Friendship Journal" and write about a different friend each day.

# WHO'S LIKE YOU?

After children identify personal characteristics and preferences, they can connect with a classmate with similar interests.

**You will need:**   paper
pencils and pens

**Directions:**

```
Juliana
a. Brown   Sammy
b. 6       Rachel
c. October Zoie
d. horse   Twan
e. Watermelon Tim
```

1. Ask the children to copy the questions below on a sheet of paper and answer them.

   a. What color are your eyes?
   b. How many people are in your family?
   c. In what month were you born?
   d. What's your favorite pet?
   e. What's your favorite food?
   f. Who is your favorite musician?
   g. Who is your favorite author?
   h. What's your favorite television show?
   i. What sport do you enjoy?
   j. What do you want to be when you grow up?

2. After the children answer the questions, let them go around the room with their papers and try to find a classmate who has answered a question in the same way. Classmates sign each other's papers next to their similar responses.

3. Children continue trying to find a classmate whose answer matches theirs for each question on their list.

4. Conclude by having the children discuss who is most like them.

**Variations:**

✎ Photocopy the questions for each child.

✎ Adapt this activity with simpler questions for younger children and more complicated questions for older children.

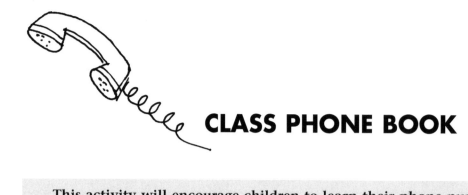

# CLASS PHONE BOOK

This activity will encourage children to learn their phone numbers and will foster friendships outside of school.

**You will need:**

front and back covers from an old phone book

paper

markers or crayons

hole punch

two book rings

**Directions:**

1. Ask each child to print his or her name at the top of a piece of paper. Then ask them to print their phone number on the bottom of the page. (An adult will need to do this for younger children.)

2. Let the children draw their pictures in the middle of the page.

3. Put the children's papers between the front and back covers of an old phone book.

4. Punch two holes in the left-hand side and attach the pages together with book rings.

5. Place the phone book by a play phone in the classroom, and let the children take turns calling each other.

6. Provide paper and markers or crayons so children can write their friends' numbers and call them at home.

**Variations:**

✆ Make a photocopy of the phone book for each child in the room to take home.

✆ Use photographs of the children to make a phone book.

✆ Model telephone etiquette with a play phone. Have the children act out how to answer the phone properly, how to make a phone call, and how to ask someone to hold. Safety on the phone should also be addressed.

**Hint:**

If children do not have a home phone, use the school's phone number.

# THE "GUESS WHO?" RIDDLE BOOK

Children will have fun reading riddles about each other, and their writing skills will be reinforced.

**You will need:**
one white envelope for each child
hole punch
photos of the children
3" × 5" index cards or paper
glue
one-inch book ring

**Directions:**

1. Give each child an envelope and ask him or her to write a riddle or description of himself or herself on it. (Younger children can dictate this to an adult.) They might include a physical description, favorite foods, hobbies, etc.

2. Have the children glue their photo to the index card and insert it in the envelope.

3. Punch a hole in the upper left-hand corner of each envelope; then put them together with the book ring. (A ribbon or piece of yarn can also be used to attach the envelopes.)

4. Read the riddle book with the children. Pull out the card in the envelope to check their answer to the description.

**Variations:**

✆ If you don't have photos of the children, just let them draw their picture on the index cards.

✆ Use this book idea to make other riddle books, writing the answer on a card and inserting it in the envelope.

# "HELLO" AND "GOOD-BYE" BOOKS

Changing schools in the middle of the year can be a traumatic experience for children. These books will help welcome new friends and be a keepsake for old friends.

**You will need:**
construction paper
drawing paper
crayons or markers
stapler

**Directions:**

1. When new children join your class during the year, tell them you would like to make a book for them to help them get to know their new friends.

2. Give each child in the class a piece of paper and ask them to draw a picture of themselves and to write their name and something special about themselves. (Younger children can dictate this to an adult.)

3. Fold the construction paper in half and write "Welcome (child's name)" on the cover. Let the new child decorate the cover.

4. Have the class present their pictures to their new friend. Then staple the pictures in the construction paper to make a book.

5. Assign one child to be a "special buddy" to show the new friend around.

**Variations:**

✏ Before a child moves away, have classmates draw a picture for their friend. Then staple the pictures together to make a "good-bye" book.

✏ If children are absent for a long period of time, have the class make them a "get well" book or banner.

✏ Teach the class this song:

> Make new friends,
> but keep the old.
> One is silver
> and the other gold.

# SECRET FRIEND

***You will need:*** small pieces of paper
box or hat

***Directions:***

1. Give each child a small piece of paper and ask them to write their names on it. Collect them in a box or hat.

2. Tell the children that they will each get to draw the name of a classmate to be their "secret pal." Explain how secret pals do nice deeds for each other, such as drawing them pictures, writing notes, or making them things. Let the children suggest other nice things they could do for their secret friend. Remind them that they must be very secretive, though, so their secret friend won't figure out who they are.

3. Pass the box or hat around and let each child draw the name of a friend.

4. At the end of a week or two of having secret friends, plan a friendship party and let the children reveal whose special friend they have been.

***Variation:*** ✎ Use secret friends around holidays or at the end of the school year. You might have Secret Santas, Special Cupids, Leprechaun Pals, or End-of-Year Buddies.

# TALENT SHOW

Allowing children to perform in front of each other fosters their esteem, builds their confidence, and encourages respect for each other.

**You will need:**
aluminum foil
toilet paper roll
markers
paper

**Directions:**

1. Talk to the children about putting on a talent show. Tell them they may sing a song, dance, do stunts, lip sync, tell jokes, etc. They may do something individually or with a group. (Also, ask for a volunteer to be the emcee.)

2. Give the children several days to plan for the event.

3. Make a pretend microphone for the emcee by wrapping aluminum foil around a toilet paper roll. Move the furniture around in the classroom to make a stage and seating area. Let the children make pretend tickets for the talent show.

4. Allow the emcee to introduce the different acts in the talent show.

5. Close the show by commenting on how many different talents were represented, and how we all have different abilities and gifts.

**Variations:**

✏ Invite another class to see the talent show.

✏ Video the show for children to take home and share with their families.

✏ Let the children put on plays that relate to different units of study, or have them dramatize various folk tales or books.

✏ Serve popcorn or another special snack after the talent show.

# ADOPTION PROGRAM

An adoption program can enhance older children's self-esteem by giving them experience in helping others. Younger children will enjoy the attention from the older student and will be provided with a good model.

**You will need:**   no materials are needed

**Directions:**

1. A class of younger children and a class of older children should be paired for this project. For example, a kindergarten class could be partners with a fourth-grade class, a second-grade class with a sixth-grade class, etc.

2. Match an older child with a younger child in each class to be "special buddies."

3. Plan weekly or monthly visits that last 30 to 45 minutes. Older children might make books for their little friends, put on a puppet show, take them on a nature walk, play games, etc. Younger children could sing songs for the older students, make an art project for them, prepare a snack, etc.

4. Be creative to make this a fun and meaningful time when children of different ages can learn and plan together.

**Variations:**

✏ Create a "story buddy" program where older and younger children read together.

✏ Set up a tutoring program or mentoring program where older children can help younger students with their school work or other problems.

# BUDDY DAY

The importance of having a friend, being a friend, and having fun with friends will be celebrated on Buddy Day.

**You will need:**
old deck of cards or magazine pictures

lunch bags, ice cream cones, pretzels, fish crackers, raisins, O-shaped cereal, peanuts

tape recorder and dance music

beanbags

art materials

paper, pencils, envelopes

blocks

board games, library books

**Directions:**

1. Several days ahead of time, announce that your class is going to have a special day called Buddy Day. On that day everyone will get to do lots of special activities with a friend. Let the children suggest things that are fun to do with a friend and use their input in planning.

2. On Buddy Day, take old playing cards or magazine pictures and cut them in half. (You will need one half for each child in the room.) Randomly pass out the picture halves. Have the children walk around and match their pictures to find their "buddy." (You might want to discuss being a good sport and having fun with whomever becomes your new buddy.)

3. Place numerals around the room. Then let the children go to the different centers and do the activities with their buddy. Here are a few ideas:

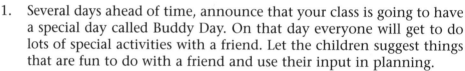
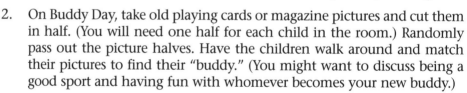
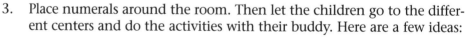

   a. Build something in the Block Center with your buddy.

   b. Make something in the Art Center with your buddy.

   c. Play the music and do a dance with your buddy.

   d. Write a letter to your buddy.

   e. Toss the beanbag to your buddy.

   f. Make a friendship snack. Put a spoonful of pretzels, fish crackers, raisins, and cereal in the bag. Shake it up. Pour the snack mix in the ice cream cone and eat it.

   g. Play a game with your buddy.

   h. Look at a book with your buddy.

**Variation:**
✏ Plan outdoor activities for children to do with their buddies.

# MAY I PLAY?

By role-playing and modeling positive behaviors, children can develop social skills for getting involved in play situations.

**You will need:**    dolls or toy animals

**Directions:**

1. Show the children the dolls. Make a group of the dolls; then set one apart from the group.

2. Begin telling a story similar to the one below:

"One day some of the dolls were playing together. Here's Carla all by herself. She wanted to play with the other dolls, so she just went over and pushed her way in and said, "Let me play!" Of course, the other dolls were angry and said, "You can't play with us." Carla walked away feeling angry and sorry for herself.

3. Ask the children to think of better ways Carla could ask to play. Let them take the doll and role-play what they would do.

**Variations:**

✏ Use dolls and toys in role-play to help model other appropriate behaviors for children.

✏ Model for children how to join a play group. Demonstrate how to observe for a few minutes, then offer to become a part of the play by helping them build or by becoming another character in the dramatic play.

# STORY STICK

**Children will develop language skills and use their imagination as they learn to build a story with their friends.**

**You will need:**

stick
spray paint
glue, glitter

**Directions:**

1.  Let the children help you find a stick on the playground. Spray paint the stick and decorate it with glitter.

2.  Gather the children in a circle and show them the "story stick." Explain that you will pass the stick around the circle and whoever is holding it may add to the story.

3.  Begin a story using one of the starters below:

    I found an old lamp and rubbed it. Out came a Genie! . . .

    One morning I went outside and jelly beans were falling from the sky! . . .

    There was a giant egg on the playground and it cracked open! . . .

4.  Encourage each child to hold the story stick and add to the story.

5.  Bring closure to the story when the stick returns to you.

**Variations:**

✏ Tape record the story as the children tell it. Then play it back for them.

✏ Ask children to say something positive about themselves or a friend as the stick is passed around.

✏ Relate the story to a holiday or classroom theme.

✏ Change the ending of a traditional tale and let the children extend it. Perhaps the Three Pigs could invite the Wolf in for pizza, or Goldilocks could take Baby Bear home with her.

**Hint:**

Carefully supervise glitter with young children, or substitute with glitter pens.

# SCHOOL SPIRIT SONG

This song will build a feeling of community in the classroom, while giving the children an opportunity to move around and release wiggles. It also fosters children's pride in their school.

**You will need:**     no materials are needed

**Directions:**

1.  Have the children stand.

2.  Begin singing and demonstrating the motions to the song "I've Got School Spirit," sung to the tune "Wheels on the Bus":

> I've got that (name of school) feeling
>> In my head,
>> In my head,              (*Point to head as you sing.*)
>> In my head,
> I've got that (name of school) feeling
>> In my head,
>> Here to stay.
>
> I've got that (school) feeling
>> In my hands . . .          (*Shake hands.*)
>> In my hips . . .           (*Wiggle hips.*)
>> In my heart . . .          (*Point to heart.*)
>> All over me . . .          (*Wiggle and shake whole body.*)

3.  Let the children suggest other body parts and movements for the song.

**Variation:**

✐  Sing the song below to the tune of "Father Abraham" as you add different body parts.

> (Name of school) has many friends.
> And there are many friends at (name of school).
> I am one of them, and so are you,
> So let's all give a cheer.
> Right hand. (*Start moving your right hand.*)
>
> And left hand, right foot, left foot, and nod your head.
> End with "Turn around and sit down."

# THE "I LIKE YOU" SONG

This is a catchy song that will capture children's attention and build feelings of friendship.

**You will need:**  no materials are needed

**Directions:**

1. Sing the song to begin a group activity or while waiting in line:

"I Like You"                    (*Tune: "Flies in the Buttermilk"*)

| | |
|---|---|
| I like you | (*Point to self, then a friend.*) |
| There's no doubt about it. | (*Shake head no.*) |
| I like you | (*Point to self, then a friend.*) |
| There's no doubt about it. | (*Shake head no.*) |
| I like you | (*Point to self, then a friend.*) |
| There's no doubt about it. | (*Shake head no.*) |
| You are my good friend. | (*Point to friend.*) |

2. Tell the children to point to a friend as they sing this second verse:

| | |
|---|---|
| You like me | (*Point to friend, then self.*) |
| There's no doubt about it. | (*Shake head no.*) |
| You like me | (*Point to friend, then self.*) |
| There's no doubt about it. | (*Shake head no.*) |
| You like me | (*Point to friend, then self.*) |
| There's no doubt about it. | (*Shake head no.*) |
| I am your good friend. | (*Point to self.*) |

**Variation:**

✏ Have children find a partner and skip around the room as they sing. After singing each verse, ask children to find a new partner to skip, jump, gallop, tiptoe, or hop with.

# WE REALLY LIKE YOU

This song emphasizes positive qualities of friends and fosters social behavior. In addition, when children wear a positive word, they are more likely to act that way.

**You will need:**

3″ × 5″ index cards or paper

markers

tape

box

**Directions:**

1. Have the children tell you words that describe good friends, such as "helpful," "friendly," "kind," and so forth. Write these words on the chalkboard or a chart tablet as they say them.

2. Write one of the words on each index card. (You may have to use each word twice to make enough for all the children in the room.)

3. Put the cards in the box, then let one child at a time pull out a card as the class sings "We Really Like You" to the tune of "We Wish You a Merry Christmas":

   We like you because you're (<u>insert word</u>).
   We like you because you're (<u>insert word</u>).
   We like you because you're (<u>insert word</u>).
   We really like you.

4. Tape the word to the child and let them wear it the rest of the day. Remind them to think about what their card says and to act that way!

**Variations:**

✎ Let the children choose their own words that they would like to wear.

✎ Have children write stories or draw pictures that are an example of their word.

# FRIENDSHIP BUBBLE

You can create a unique environment in your classroom with the bubble. Think of all the possibilities it can grow into from a theme or unit!

***You will need:***

two plastic 9′ × 12′ painting tarps

one roll duct tape

one box fan (ask parents to lend an old one)

***Directions:***

1. Cut the tarps into two 8′ × 10′ rectangles. Put aside the extra tarp to use later.

2. Lay the two rectangles on top of each other on the floor and tape together all around with duct tape.

3. To make a door, cut a 4-foot slit in the middle of a long side. Reinforce the slit with tape.

4. Next, make a tunnel to get the air into the bubble from the fan. Take the extra tarp (left over from cutting) and tape it around the front of the fan to make a tunnel. (Overlap ends and tape.)

5. Cut slit (approximately 2′ long) in the middle of one of the short sides. Tape the open end to the tunnel in the slit.

6. Place the bubble in a quiet area of the room with the back of the fan next to a wall.

7. Turn on the fan and watch the bubble inflate. (You might need to prop the fan on a large cement or wooden block to get more air into the bubble.)

8. Allow several children at a time to get in the bubble to read, talk, play board games, etc.

***Variations:***

✏ Add pillows, books, or magazines to create a reading bubble.

✏ Create different scenes in the bubble to relate to classroom units or seasons. Snowflakes could be hung from the ceiling to make a winter wonderland; stuffed animals and green streamers to create a jungle; fish to make an ocean, etc. Add a tape recorder and theme music to the bubble.

***Hint:*** Use this activity with older children and supervise carefully.

# CLASS BOOKS

Reading and writing skills will flourish as children contribute to class books.

***You will need:***   paper
construction paper
crayons, markers
stapler

***Directions:***

1. Give each child a piece of paper on which to draw a picture for one of the books below.

   <u>The Best Day Ever</u>
   <u>If I Were the Teacher</u>
   <u>Dear Mr. President</u>
   <u>Changing Places</u>    (Whom you'd like to change
   <u>The Day All Animals Talked</u>       places with.)
   <u>My Biggest Nightmare</u>
   <u>If I had a Magic Wish</u>
   <u>My Life as a Fish</u>

2. Let the children write or dictate sentences to go along with their pictures.

3. Staple the pages together between construction paper to make a book. Allow the children to decorate the cover.

***Variations:***

✏ Place the books in your classroom library and let the children "check" them out to take home.

✏ Insert children's pictures and stories in sheet protectors or a magnetic photo album to make a book.

# BUDDY SYSTEM

**Friendships will be strengthened, children will learn how to help each other, and they will learn how to work out their own problems with the buddy system.**

*You will need:*      no materials are needed

*Directions:*

1. Have a class meeting to discuss creating a buddy system. Explain that children will be paired with a friend so that when they have a problem or need help, they will have someone to turn to.

2. Role-play situations where children might use their buddy. For example, getting help to tie their shoes, assistance with a game or assignment, or a hug when they're upset.

3. Pair children with complementary strengths and weaknesses. You might pair a child who has good academic skills with a child who has difficulty, or a shy child with an outgoing child.

4. When a child comes to you for help, suggest he or she checks with his or her buddy first.

5. Have class meeting frequently so children can share how their buddies are helping them.

*Variations:*

✐   Use buddies on field trips or to work on classroom projects.

✐   Rotate buddies as appropriate to foster new friendships.

✐   Develop a mentoring program in your school where teachers or older students tutor, counsel, and support children who are at risk.

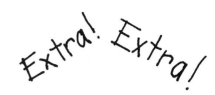

# CLASS NEWS AND VIEWS

Children will develop reading and writing skills as they find an outlet for some of their feelings and acknowledge classmates' accomplishments.

***You will need:***
newspaper
cloth tape
stapler
newsprint or butcher paper
scissors
markers, crayons, or paints

***Directions:***

1. Trim a sheet of newspaper so that it is 18" × 24".

2. Cut newsprint or butcher paper the same size and staple it in the newspaper to make a book.

3. Cover the staples with cloth tape to make a binding on the book.

4. Write "Class News" on the cover with markers.

5. Show the book to the children and explain that when they have some news to share with the class, they can write it in the book. They can also draw a picture, write a story, make a suggestion, or say "thank you" to a friend in the book.

6. Place the book in your Writing Center or library, along with crayons and markers.

7. Share the "Class News" daily with the children before they go home in the afternoon.

***Variations:***

✏ Choose one or two children each day to be "class reporters" and to write down news in the book.

✏ Let the children interview each other and put their papers in the "Class News."

# GROUPING GAMES

It's important to vary the children in groups so they have the opportunity to get to know each other. Try some of these unique games to randomly group children.

*You will need:*
playing cards or greeting cards
colored dots
hard candy

*Directions:*

1. *Puzzles* — Take old greeting cards or playing cards and cut them into puzzles. (Cut into as many pieces as members you want in each group.) Pass out a puzzle piece to each child. Then have them try to find the rest of their group by matching their pieces.

2. *Dots* — Let each child select a colored dot or sticker. Have people with like colors form a group.

3. *Flavors* — Ask each child to select his or her favorite flavor of hard candy. Children have to move around showing their candy to each other until they've found a group with like colors. (Fruit, candy bars, and other types of food can also be used.)

4. *Snap* — Whisper in each child's ear a certain number of times to snap, such as once, twice, three, or four times. Children begin snapping and move around until they find others snapping that same number of times. Be sure the children rest between each grouping of snaps.

5. *Tunes* — Give each child a simple tune to hum ("Happy Birthday," "Twinkle, Twinkle Little Star," "London Bridge," "Farmer in the Dell," etc.). Children try to form a group based on similar tunes they are humming. (You can do a similar activity by having children make different animal sounds.)

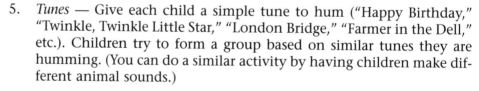

# STORY BAGS

Story bags enable children to work together as they use their imagination and language skills.

**You will need:**
lunch bags

paper clips, rubber bands, crayons, pencils, balloons, blocks, and other common objects and toys

**Directions:**

1. Put four or five different objects in each bag.

2. Divide the children into groups of four. (Have them count off, draw numbers, etc.)

3. Give each group a bag and tell them to dump out their objects and look at them.

4. Challenge the children to make up a story using all the objects in their bag.

5. Let the groups take turns telling their stories to the rest of the class.

**Variations:**

- Exchange the bags and ask the groups to come up with different stories using the props.

- Have each child look in his or her desk or cubby and find one object. Divide the children into groups and ask them to make up a story using their various items.

- Ask older children to write their stories.

- Place magazine pictures in bags and challenge children to create a story from the pictures.

# MAIL TIME

Writing skills and friendships will be enhanced with a mail system in your classroom.

**You will need:**
scrap paper and other types of paper
envelopes
self-stick notepads
carbon paper
rubber stamps and pad
one 5″ × 8″ or 9″ × 12″ clasp envelope for each child
red construction paper
brad fasteners
crayons, pencils, markers
tape, scissors, glue

**Directions:**

1. Give each child a clasp envelope from which to construct a mail pouch. Tell the children to write their name on it and decorate it with their picture.

2. Cut out small flags from the red construction paper and let the children attach them to their mail pouch with a brad fastener.

3. Staple the mail pouches to a bulletin board or tape them to a wall or shelf.

4. Set up a Writing Center with the above materials and let the children write letters to each other and deliver them in their mail pouches.

**Variations:**

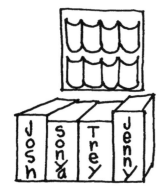

- ✏ Photocopy children's photos and let them glue their friends' photos to envelopes instead of writing their names.

- ✏ Use a vinyl shoe rack to store writing materials.

- ✏ Ask each child to bring in an empty cereal box. Let the children decorate the boxes, writing their name down the sides. Line up the boxes and use to hold letters they write to each other.

- ✏ Contact the Postal Service about the in-school postal program they offer called "Wee Deliver."

Literacy Initiatives
Corporate Relations
U.S. Postal Service
475 L'Enfant Plaza, SW, Room 10541
Washington, D.C. 20260-3100

# THREE CHEERS

Emphasize supporting classmates with "three cheers," a "round of applause," and a "mini-celebration."

***You will need:***  no materials are needed

***Directions:***

1. When a child does something special or helpful, get the other children to join you in this cheer:

    > Three cheers for (child's name).
    > Hip, hip, hooray!  *(Hold first in the air.)*
    > Hip, hip, hooray!
    > Hip, hip, hooray!

2. Lead the children in a "round" of applause for a classmate by clapping your hands in front of you in a circular motion.

3. Demonstrate how to applaud for classmates in sign language. Hold hands in the air and shake them around.

4. Have a "mini-celebration" to support students. Snap fingers up and down in front of you.

***Variations:***

- Try a "ketchup bottle" clap. Make a fist with one hand; then hit down on it with the other hand open (as if trying to get ketchup to come out).

- An "opera applause" can be produced by tapping index fingers together.

- Do the "fish clap" by flapping outstretched hands over and under each other.

- Let the children make up their own unique ways to cheer for their classmates.

# THE "THANK-YOU" BOARD

Children will be encouraged to do favors for their friends, and friends will have a visible way of showing their appreciation. This activity also fosters writing skills.

**You will need:**

large sheet of posterboard

markers

tape

**Directions:**

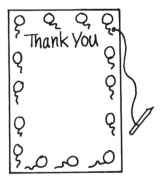

1. Print "Thank You!" at the top of the board and decorate with happy faces and balloons.

2. Tape it to the classroom door or another prominent place in the room.

3. Ask the children to give you examples of nice things friends can do for each other. Explain that when someone does something nice for them, they can write that person's name along with a note or picture on the "thank-you" board.

5. Call attention to the board once a day. Ask children to elaborate on a kindness shown to them.

**Variations:**

✏ Use a dry-erase board, a portion of your chalkboard, or a bulletin board as a "thank-you" location.

✏ Vary the "thank-you" board with the season. It might be the "apple of my eye" in September, "snowing with good deeds" in January, or "blooming with kindness" in April.

✏ Provide children with cut-out shapes or small note cards on which to write "thank you's" to their friends.

# CLASS RULES

Learning to follow classroom rules will help children feel secure because they will know what behavior is expected of them. This activity is especially helpful at the beginning of the school year.

*You will need:*    chart paper or posterboard
markers

*Directions:*

1. Bring the class together for a discussion on school rules.

2. Explain that rules help everyone know what they can and cannot do. Discuss what would happen if there were no rules.

3. Write "Class Rules" at the top of the chart paper. Write the rules that the children suggest. (Try to state them positively so children know what behavior is expected of them.)

 **Class Rules**

1. Be kind to friends.
2. Keep your hands to yourself.
3. Respect school materials.
4. Walk in the hall.

4. Post the rules in a prominent place in the classroom and review them daily until the children are familiar with them. If a child is not doing what he or she should do, call his or her attention to the rule.

5. Compliment the children on good behavior and emphasize how nice it is for the whole group when everyone does his or her job.

*Variations:*

✍ Have the children decorate the rule chart.

✍ Divide children into small groups and allow them to make their own rules and posters.

✍ Make a book of class rules. Have each child draw a picture of a rule and write a sentence to go along with it. Put their pictures together to make a book.

# LET'S VOTE

Going along with the majority is the basis of a democratic system and an effective way to help children learn to cooperate and negotiate.

**You will need:**
large appliance box
utility knife
paper and pencils
shoe box
markers

**Directions:**

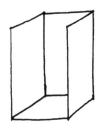

1. Cut one side and the top off the box to resemble a voting booth. Let the children decorate the box with markers.

2. Cut a hole in the top of the shoe box to serve as a ballot box.

3. Give each child a piece of paper. One at a time let them go in the voting booth and make a selection. They might vote on:
   —the book they'd like read
   —the game they want to play outside
   —what they want to eat for snack
   —their favorite song to sing

(Older children can write their own choice, but younger children will need to have picture clues to mark.)

4. Have children insert their ballots in the shoe box.

5. Count the responses to determine winners.

6. Talk about why it is important for adults to vote. What happens if nobody votes? Why do we vote by "secret ballot"?

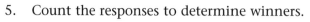

**Variation:**

➥ Whenever possible, let the children vote on issues in the classroom by raising their hands. It will give you feedback and make them feel respected and important.

**Hint:**

Be sure the children stay away from the utility knife.

# "SCHOOL IS FUN" GRAPH

This activity lets children express their favorite thing to do at school. It also develops math skills.

**You will need:**   posterboard
crayons
yardstick
markers

**Directions:**

1. Draw a grid on the posterboard similar to the one below.
2. Write "School Is Fun" at the top. Then let children suggest their favorite activities to go on the side.
3. Let each child color in the box by his or her favorite activity.
4. Compare results. Does everybody like the same thing? What's the most popular activity? The second most popular? What is the least favorite activity?

**Variations:**

✏ Recognize children's likes by setting aside a special time when they can all do their "favorite thing."

✏ Make graphs of the children's favorite games, books, songs, foods, pets, and so forth.

| School Is Fun | 1 | 2 | 3 | 4 | 5 | 6 | 7 |
|---|---|---|---|---|---|---|---|
| Art | | | | | | | |
| Reading | | | | | | | |
| Outdoor Play | | | | | | | |
| Science | | | | | | | |
| Math | | | | | | | |
| Music | | | | | | | |
| Blocks | | | | | | | |

# TEACHER OF THE DAY

Children's esteem and leadership skills will soar when they become "teacher of the day." This role-play may also give children insight into the challenging job of the teacher.

***You will need:***     planning calendar
pencil

***Directions:***

1.  Ask the children who would like to trade places with you and be the teacher. What would they do if they were the teacher? Explain that once a week you will let them take turns being the teacher for half an hour. They may plan activities, play a game, read a story, provide a snack, or do anything they would like with the class.

2.  Let each child choose a day and write their name on the calendar. (You may also draw names, go in alphabetical order, or use this as a reward.)

3.  Several days before becoming "teacher," ask children to write or tell you what they plan to do. Offer suggestions or alternatives.

4.  Have the "teacher of the day" sit at your desk. Support the "teacher" in his or her activities.

5.  Follow up by asking the children what they liked or disliked about being the teacher.

***Variation:***     ✏   Let two children share the role of teacher and plan together.

# HELPER STICKS

"Helper sticks" give every child an opportunity to develop responsibility and to share in the operation of the classroom.

**You will need:**
jumbo craft sticks
fine-tip markers
juice can
construction paper
glue
scissors
envelope

**Directions:**

1. Decorate the outside of the juice can with construction paper. Label the can "helper sticks."

2. Print each child's name on a craft stick. Then place all the sticks in the can.

3. Whenever there is a special errand to be run or a job to be done, choose a stick from the can.

4. After that child has had a turn, put his or her stick in the envelope. When all of the sticks have been used, start over again by removing the sticks from the envelope and putting them back in the can.

**Variations:**

✏ Use "helper sticks" to select classroom jobs, choose centers, or for other classroom activities.

✏ When children are doing a big job, let them choose a friend from the "helper sticks" to assist them.

# PRINCE AND PRINCESS

What fun to wear a crown and be a prince or princess! Children will also develop leadership skills and feel important.

**You will need:**
construction paper or posterboard
glitter
glue
scissors
stapler
crayons or markers

**Directions:**

1. Cut the construction paper or posterboard into 24″ × 4″ strips. (The construction paper may need to be pieced together.)

2. Cut one side to look like a crown as shown.

3. Choose one child each day to be the prince or princess. Let that child decorate his or her own crown with glitter and crayons.

4. Fit the crown to the child's head and staple the paper.

5. Announce who the prince or princess is at group time. Then let that child be line leader, perform special tasks, and be your helper all day long.

6. Allow the prince or princess to wear his or her crown home at the end of the day.

**Variations:**

✏ Ask the children what they would do if they were a real prince or princess.

✏ Use aluminum foil to cover the crown.

**Hint:**
Supervise glitter carefully with young children, or substitute with glitter pens.

# THE "CLEAN-UP CLOCK"

Cleaning up helps children develop responsibility and teaches them how to work together to accomplish a task. A timer will help them bring closure to their activities so they will clean up more cheerfully.

**You will need:**      minute timer

**Directions:**

1. When it is almost time to clean up, remind the children that you will set the "clean-up clock" for five minutes. When the timer goes off, everyone needs to work together to clean up.

2. After the buzzer goes off, sing the song below to the tune of "Heigh Ho, Heigh Ho."

> Heigh ho, heigh ho,
>    it's clean-up time we know.
> We'll do our best,
>    then help the rest.
> Heigh ho, heigh ho.

3. Remind the children there's more time to play outside or do other fun activities when everyone works together.

**Variations:**

- Set the time for five minutes and play "beat the clean-up clock" as children try to clean up the room before the buzzer goes off.

- Use a music box, train whistle, bubbles, flashlight, or other prop to get the children's attention for cleaning up.

- Choose one child to be the "white glove inspector." Give that child paper and a pencil and let him or her go around the room and make a list of areas that need to be cleaned.

- If children are reluctant to help, then give them a choice, such as, "Jamie, do you want to put away the play dough or wash the table?"

# NOT ENOUGH

Sharing will be a natural outcome of this activity. Children will also learn how to problem-solve.

**You will need:**  packages of crackers, raisins, or other food (have half as many as you need)

napkins

**Directions:**
1. Ask the children to wash their hands. Then choose a helper to pass out napkins.

2. Choose another child to pass out the food. Have the children suggest solutions when they discover there isn't enough to go around. Listen to all the possible solutions; then encourage the group to decide on the best idea.

3. Reinforce the children for solving the problem and for sharing with each other.

**Variations:**

- Divide children into pairs. Give each child a piece of fruit, such as a banana or an apple. Tell them that the only way they can eat the fruit is if their friend gives it to them.

- Pass out a sheet of paper and *one* crayon to each child. Explain that they may use their color or trade with a friend. When the children have finished, let them show their pictures. Talk about how colorful their pictures are because they learned to share.

# FRIENDLY SALAD

This friendly salad will be a tasty treat and will emphasize the positive outcome from working together and sharing.

**You will need:**

fruit
large bowl
safety knives
serving spoon
cups and spoons for the children

**Directions:**

1. Several days before making the friendly salad, write a note to the parents asking them to send in a fruit on a designated day.

2. Let each child wash and prepare his or her fruit by cutting it into small pieces. (*Caution:* Teach children how to use knives safely. Be sure to supervise the children.)

3. Put all the fruit together in the bowl and stir. Serve the fruit salad in cups.

4. After eating the fruit, talk about how it tasted. Would they prefer a single fruit, or was it better with lots of fruit mixed together? Why is "friendly salad" a good name for this recipe?

5. Encourage the children to talk about what happens when people work together and help each other. Ask them to give examples of how people in their family, school, and community work together for a common goal.

**Variation:**

✏ Tell the story of *Stone Soup* by Marcia Brown. Then have every child bring in a vegetable from home. Clean and prepare the vegetables; then cook them in a crock pot with several cans of bouillon and water. Oh, and don't forget the stone!

# GRAB BAG ART

Children will delight in collecting junk from around their house and passing it on to a friend. What a great way to set creativity soaring and learn about recycling!

**You will need:**    one paper lunch bag for each child
scissors, glue, and other art supplies
recycled materials

**Directions:**

1. Pass out a bag to each child. Ask them to go home and look around their house for objects that can be recycled. (Suggest objects such as cardboard rollers from paper towels, plastic bags and containers, clean aluminum foil, junk mail, magazines, and so forth.) Tell them to fill their bag with "clean" junk and bring it back to school the next day.

2. Collect the bags as the children bring them in. (Prepare a few extra for those who forget.)

3. Randomly pass out the bags. Then challenge the children to create something new from the "junk" in their bags. Have scissors, glue, tape, and other art supplies available for them to use.

4. Let the children share their finished creations with their classmates. (See if children can identify who got the bag they brought in.)

**Variations:**

✏ Have children make an invention or other object relating to a unit of study from their grab bags.

✏ Let several children put their bags together and make a group project.

✏ Keep a "junk box" in the art area with recycled materials for the children to explore and create with.

# FRIENDSHIP NECKLACE

As children make their friendship necklaces and share phone numbers with their classmates, they will be developing motor and writing skills.

**You will need:**

construction paper scraps
scissors
crayons or markers
hole punch
string, yarn, or ribbon

**Directions:**

1. Introduce this project by asking the children if they would like to have each other's phone number. Ask them to suggest when and why the would like to call their school friends. Explain that they will each get to make a "friendship necklace" so they'll have all their friends' phone numbers at home.

2. Have each child cut 3-inch shapes from the construction paper. (You may need to do this ahead of time for younger children.) They will need as many pieces of paper as there are children in the room.

3. Ask the children to write their name and phone number on each shape. Next, have the children pass these out to their friends.

4. Let the children punch holes in their shapes and string them on the yarn or ribbon. Knot the ends together to make a necklace.

5. Encourage the children to wear their necklaces home and to keep them in a safe place.

**Variations:**

✏ To save time, photocopy the children's names and phone numbers.

✏ Let the children work on this project over several days.

✏ This is a great get-acquainted activity for the beginning of the school year. Or it can be a special way to say good-bye at the end of the year.

# PAL PORTRAITS

Children will make a friend and have a laugh as they interact cooperatively drawing each other's portraits.

*You will need:*

paper
crayons or markers (body colors)
pencils

*Directions:*

1. Randomly divide children into pairs. (A good way to do this is to take old playing cards or greeting cards and cut them in half. Give each child one half, then let them match their cards to find their partner.)

2. Pass out paper, pencils, and crayons or markers. Have the children sit facing their partner as they draw each other's portrait.

3. To include the activity, let the children show each other's portrait to the class and tell one new thing they learned about their friend.

4. Display the pictures in the classroom.

*Variations:*

✏ This is a good ice-breaker for the beginning of the year. It's also fun to do on a rainy day.

✏ With a new class, assign each child a partner who he or she will get to introduce to his or her classmates. Give students several minutes to get to know each other by asking questions about their hobbies, favorite music, likes and dislikes, and so forth.

# COOPERATIVE SCULPTURE

What an exciting way to involve all the children in your classroom in creating a giant sculpture that is constantly evolving.

**You will need:**

one corrugated cardboard box (any size) for each child
tape
large paintbrushes
red, yellow, and blue paints
newspapers
plastic containers (yogurt cups or margarine tubs) for paint
smocks or old shirts

**Directions:**

1. Ask each child to bring in a cardboard box. Or ask an office supply store to save them for you.

2. Tape the boxes shut.

3. Cover the working area with newspapers and provide smocks for the children. (Or have each child bring in a parent's old shirt from home.)

4. Pour the paint in the plastic containers. Then let each child paint his or her box. Set the boxes aside to dry.

5. The next day, let the children paint designs or patterns on their boxes, and again let the boxes dry.

6. Have each child hold his or her box as he or she sits on the floor in a circle. One at a time let the children stack their boxes on top of each other's to create a sculpture. What happens when everyone works together?

7. Redesign the sculpture. How tall can the children make it? How long? Can they build a tunnel they can crawl through? Can they march around it? Can they think of a title for their sculpture?

**Variations:**

- Put the boxes in the hall with a sign that says "Please Touch." Other classes will enjoy moving the sculpture around.

- Take the boxes out to the playground on a dry day. Or use them in the Block Center.

**Hint:**

If tempera paint is used, add white glue to the paint so it won't rub off when the children play with their boxes.

# BAG CITY

Children will explore what it takes to make a community as they work together on this project. Map skills and social studies concepts will also be developed.

***You will need:***

lunch bags
newspaper
construction paper
crayons or markers
scissors
glue

***Directions:***

1. Divide the children into small groups. Ask them to make a list of the different helpers, stores, services, and other locations in their community.

2. Let the children work together to make model communities with the lunch bags using the procedure below:

   a. Draw a building with crayons or markers on one of the lunch bags. Construction paper can also be used to add detail.

   b. Stuff a second lunch bag with newspaper torn in strips.

   c. Insert the decorated sack over the stuffed bag as shown to create a 3-dimensional building.

3. Have the children arrange the bags and play with them using toy cars, small dolls, plastic animals, etc.

***Variations:***

- Let the children use classroom blocks to create a community. Label the blocks and make roads with tape on the floor.

- Divide children into small groups and ask them to draw a map of their community, neighborhood, or school.

# PEANUT BUTTER

Here's a positive way to get children up, moving, and interacting with friends.

**You will need:**   no materials are needed

**Directions:**

1. Have the children find a partner to begin this game.

2. As the teacher calls out different body parts, the children should stick those parts of their bodies together like "peanut butter." For example, the teacher might call out, "hand to hand," "back to back," "thumb to thumb," or "ankle to ankle."

3. When the teacher calls out "peanut butter," everyone must tip toe and find a new partner.

4. Continue calling out different body parts until "peanut butter" is said and everyone must find another new partner.

**Variations:**

✎ Call out two different body parts, such as "foot and elbow." The children must touch their foot to the other person's elbow.

✎ Let the children take turns being the leader and calling out body parts.

✎ Play a record or beat a drum. When the music stops, the children must find a friend and touch the body parts called.

✎ Have children face each other. One person is "it" and the other person is the mirror and must do exactly what "it" does. Switch places after several minutes.

# COOPERATIVE ART

Creativity and friendships will flourish as children work together on the following seven art projects. In addition, these "process" art activities integrate social skills, language, and pleasure.

## ROLL A PICTURE

**You will need:**
marbles or golf balls
paint
spoons
paper
empty box (shirt boxes work well)

**Directions:**

1. Line the box with a piece of paper.

2. Let the children drop the marbles or golf balls in the paint. Then put them in the box with the spoon.

3. Two children hold the box between them and roll the box back and forth to create a painting.

**Variation:**

✏ Use rocks, toy cars, or other objects to roll around in the box.

## SHAVING CREAM PAINTING

**You will need:**
can of shaving cream
sponges
water

**Directions:**

1. Have several children stand around a table with a washable surface.

2. Squirt a large pile of shaving cream in front of each of them and challenge them to cover the table with it.

3. When children are tired of painting with the shaving cream, let them wash it off with sponges and water. The room will smell good, the table will be clean, and so will the children's hands!

# DOTS

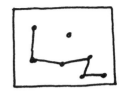

***You will need:***   paper
crayons

***Directions:***

1. Give each child a sheet of paper and instruct the children to make ten dots on it with a crayon.

2. Have the children exchange their papers with a friend.

3. Tell the children to connect the dots on their page and create an object or design out of it.

# CLASS QUILT

***You will need:***   white paper towels
four small cups
food colorings
cloth tape
water

***Directions:***

1. Fill the cups halfway with water. Add several squirts of food coloring to each cup.

2. Give each child a paper towel and demonstrate how to fold it into a small square.

3. Let the children dip each corner of their paper towel into a different color of food coloring. Have them carefully unfold it and hang it to dry.

4. Tape the paper towels together to make a large wall hanging or quilt.

***Variations:***

✏ Have children draw individual pictures of their favorite book or animal. Punch holes in the corners and tie them together with yarn to make a quilt.

✏ Make an alphabet quilt by giving each child a different letter to illustrate. Tape or tie their papers together with yarn.

✏ Use squares of muslin or old sheets and let the children decorate them with fabric crayons or permanent markers. Sew together to make a quilt to hang in the classroom or hallway.

# Junk Sculpture

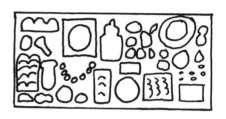

**You will need:**

foam board or corrugated cardboard

glue gun

"junk" such as plastic containers, detergent bottles, egg cartons, film containers, lids, old toys, plastic packages, bottle caps, etc.

spray paint

**Directions:**

1. Have the children collect "junk" from home and bring it in for about a week.

2. Let them arrange the objects on the foam board or cardboard. Challenge them to squeeze as many on as they can.

3. Glue the objects in place with a glue gun. (An adult will need to do this.)

4. Spray paint over the entire sculpture. (*Caution:* Keep the children away from the spray paint.)

5. Hang on the wall.

**Variation:**

✏ Let the children paint cardboard tubes from toilet paper, wrapping paper, and paper towels that have been cut in different lengths. Glue to a piece of corrugated cardboard to create a sculpture that can be hung on the wall or that can sit on a shelf.

# Pass It On

**You will need:**

crayons

paper

**Directions:**

1. Give each child a sheet of paper and tell the children to begin drawing a picture of anything they like. (Remind them to write their name on the back.)

2. After several minutes. tell them to pass it to their friend sitting beside them. Children draw on their friend's picture several minutes until you tell them to pass it to another friend.

3. After 10 to 15 minutes, tell the children to return the pictures to their original owners.

4. Discuss how the final picture varies from the owner's original drawing.

# HANDY ART

**You will need:**

construction paper

paint

scissors

butcher paper

glue

crayons and markers

**Directions:**

1. Have the children trace around their hands on construction paper and cut them out.

2. Use their handprints to create one of the designs below.

Tree

Sunshine

Rainbow

Holiday Symbols

Footprints

**Variations:**

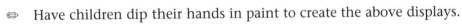

- Have children dip their hands in paint to create the above displays.

- Use handprints to make a bulletin board of a "Hand-some Class." Have each child trace around their hand and cut it out. In the palm, ask them to draw their face. In each finger they should write some personal information, such as the number of people in their family, pets, favorite books, hobbies, etc.

121

# PARTNER GAMES

The following eight games and stunts will encourage children to cooperate as they play and have fun.

## SCULPTURES

***You will need:***    no materials are needed

***Directions:***

1. Divide children into pairs. One child is the "clay" and the other child is the "sculptor."

2. The "sculptor" moves the other child's arms, legs, head, and other body parts into different positions to create a statue.

3. Have the children change places.

***Variation:***    ✏ Divide the children into small groups and challenge them to create a statue in which they are all connected.

## DRIVING DERBY

***You will need:***    music

***Directions:***

1. Divide the children into pairs.

2. Have one child stand in front and bend his or her elbows. The second child stands behind and puts his or her hands on the first child's elbows.

3. The first child is the "car" and the second child is the "driver" who will steer the "car" around the room when the music starts.

4. Change places when the music stops.

# ROW YOUR BOAT

*You will need:*  no materials are needed

*Directions:*

1. Divide children into pairs and have them sit on the floor with their legs extended so their feet are touching.
2. Demonstrate how to grasp each other's hands and lean back and forth as if rowing a boat.
3. Sing "Row, Row, Row Your Boat" as children move to the beat.

*Variation:*  ✏ Row the boats slowly, medium, fast, and then "speed boat."

# RACKET BALL

*You will need:*  clothes hangers
old hose
balloons or sponge balls
tape

*Directions:*

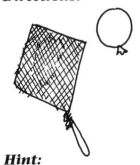

1. Stretch the hanger so it is shaped like a diamond.
2. Stretch one leg of the hose over the hanger and knot it at the bottom.
3. Bend up the hook on the hanger and tape it to make a handle.
4. Let the children use the hangers like rackets and "bat" the balloon or sponge ball back and forth to each other.

*Hint:*  Balloons should not be used with young children.

# TOWEL TOSS

*You will need:*  large towels
stuffed animals

*Directions:*

1. Divide children into pairs.
2. Give each pair a towel and a stuffed animal or other toy.
3. Children hold the ends of the towel and gently toss the toy up and down.

# SOUND DETECTIVES

**You will need:** no materials are needed

**Directions:**

*Eeee!*
*Grrrr!*
*Ssss!*

1. Divide the children into two teams.

2. Instruct one child on each team to act like a particular animal, such as a lion, elephant, monkey, and so forth.

3. Children move around and make their sound and motion until they find the person on the other team who is their partner.

**Variation:**

✏ Pets, book characters, and other objects can be used.

# MUSICAL "SHARES"

**You will need:** tape or record
chairs

**Directions:**

1. Arrange the chairs facing alternating directions. There should be one less chair than the number of children playing the game.

2. Tell the children to march around the chairs as you play the music. When the music stops, they must all find a chair and sit on it. If a child can't find a chair to sit on, then they must share with a friend.

3. Continue playing the game, removing a chair each time the music stops.

4. Children should end up giggling as they all try to "share" one chair.

# TOSS AND SCOOP

**You will need:** plastic milk jugs (ask each child to bring one in)
newspaper
masking tape, scissors
foam balls

**Directions:**

1. Cut off the top and side of the milk jugs (as shown) with scissors to make a scoop.

2. Make newspaper balls by wadding up a sheet of newspaper and wrapping masking tape around it.

3. Divide children into pairs. Let them take turns throwing the ball so their partner can catch it in their scoop.

# MOVING AND SINGING WITH FRIENDS

These four activities develop motor skills, language, cooperation, and, above all, friendships.

## THE MORE WE GET TOGETHER

**You will need:**    no materials are needed

**Directions:**

1. Have the children put their arms around each other's shoulders as they sway and sing the song below.

   "The More We Get Together" (*Tune:* "Lassie and Laddie")

   The more we get together, together, together.
   The more we get together the happier we'll be.
   For your friends are my friends,
   And my friends are your friends.
   The more we get together the happier we'll be.

2. Tell the children to "scramble" and find other friends to put their arms around as you sing the song again.

## EVERYBODY SHAKE A HAND

**You will need:**    no materials are needed

**Directions:**

1. Sing the song below as children walk around and shake hands with each other.

   "Everybody Shake a Hand" (*Tune:* "Buffalo Gal")

   Everybody shake a hand, shake a hand,
      shake a hand.
   Everybody shake a hand and
      walk around the room.

2. On the second verse, sing "Everybody give high five. . ."

3. On the third verse, sing "Everybody scratch a back. . ."

4. End with "Everybody hug a friend, hug a friend, hug a friend. Everybody hug a friend, then walk back to your seat."

# MOVING MACHINE

**You will need:**     no materials are needed

**Directions:**

1.  Instruct the children to think of a motion and a sound that might go with it.

2.  One child at a time stands up and begins making his or her motion and sound.

3.  The next child touches the first child, then adds his or her motion and sound.

4.  Continue adding, one child at a time, making sure they touch the previous child before they make their motion and sound.

5.  In the end the entire class becomes the "moving machine."

# FRIENDSHIP TRAIN

**You will need:**     no materials are needed

**Directions:**

1.  Have the children sit or stand in a circle.

2.  Choose one child to be the train and "chug" around the room as this song is sung:

    "I have a Friend" (*Tune:* "Little Liza Jane")

    I have a friend who you all know and
      (child's name) is his/her name.
    I have a friend who you all know and
      (child's name) is his/her name.
    Get on board little children,
    Get on board little children,
    Get on board little children,
    There's room for many more.

3.  The first child chooses a friend to join the train. The second child puts his or her hands on the first child's shoulders as they "chug" around singing the song with the second child's name.

4.  Continue until all the children in the room are part of the train.

# 3

# Feelings and Emotions

It is important for children to recognize their feelings and emotions, and learn how to deal with them in acceptable ways. Through art projects, songs, writing activities, and other creative experiences presented in this section, children will learn that everyone has different emotions and feelings—and that's okay!

# THE "HOW DO YOU FEEL?" BOOK

This activity will help children verbalize some of the feelings they have and will provide them with acceptable ways of dealing with these emotions.

**You will need:**

two pieces of 22" × 28" posterboard
scissors
markers
two book rings

**Directions:**

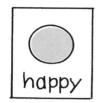

1.  Cut the posterboard into fourths. (You should have eight pieces that measure 14" × 11".)

2.  Cut a 7-inch circle out of the middle of six sheets.

3.  Write a different emotion under each circle as shown. Use words such as happy, sad, angry, proud, afraid, embarrassed, surprised, loved.

4.  Make front and back covers for the book from the remaining two pieces of posterboard. Print "How Do You Feel? on the front cover and let the children decorate it.

5.  Punch two holes at the bottom of each page; then put the pages together with book rings.

6.  Introduce the book by talking about how we all have different kinds of feelings and that's okay. Let the children take turns putting their head through the holes on the pages and making an appropriate facial expression.

7.  Encourage the children to talk about what makes them feel that way. Discuss positive responses for dealing with each of these feelings. For example, "What makes you angry? Should you hit someone when you are angry? What is a better thing to do? What else can you do if you're angry?"

**Variation:**

✏ Take the facial expressions out of the book and use them in songs and skits.

# HAPPY, HAPPY ME

Children will learn to identify different feelings that they have as they discover that it's okay to feel different ways.

**You will need:**

posterboard or heavy paper

craft sticks

scissors

markers or crayons

glue

copy of pictures on the following two pages

**Directions:**

1. Copy the facial expressions and glue them to posterboard or heavy paper. (Color them with markers or crayons if you desire.)

2. Cut out each face and glue it to a craft stick.

3. Hold up each expression as you say the poem below:

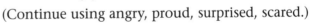

Happy, Happy
   happy, happy me.
But sometimes
I'm a sad me.

Sad, sad,
   sad, sad me.
But sometimes
   I'm an angry me.

(Continue using angry, proud, surprised, scared.)

All of these feelings
   that you see
Are emotions
   that belong to me!

4. Let the children take the puppets and describe what makes them feel that way.

**Variations:**

- Use wiggly eyes, yarn, and other craft materials to decorate the faces.

- Make other expressions, such as shy, embarrassed, sleepy, and so forth.

# Facial Expressions

HAPPY

ANGRY

SCARED

SAD

PROUD

SURPRISED

© 1997 by John Wiley & Sons

130

# FACIAL EXPRESSIONS

SLEEPY

SILLY

GROUCHY

CURIOUS

SHY

MAKE YOUR OWN

# AFRICAN VILLAGE SONG

This multicultural song comes from Africa and reinforces the fact that everyone has good days and bad days.

**You will need:**  no materials are needed

**Directions:**

1. Tell the children that there are some places in Africa and other parts of the world where it is very dry and they seldom get any rain. Sometimes there isn't even enough water to grow food to eat; then there is a famine. When it finally rains, it makes the people very happy because they know that soon the sun will shine and the flowers will bloom. The flowers make them happy because they know that they will soon be able to grow food to eat.

2. Make motions as you sing this song to the tune of "He's Got the Whole World in His Hands."

   When the rain falls down on everyone,
   the rich and poor and little ones.
   When the rain falls down on everyone
   there will soon be sun.

   When the sun shines down on everyone,
   the rich and poor and little ones.
   When the sun shines down from the sky
   flowers bloom by and by.

   When the flowers bloom for everyone,
   the rich and poor and little ones.
   When the flowers bloom all around,
   food will grow from the ground.

3. Ask the children how they think people feel when it doesn't rain and they have nothing to eat. How do they feel when they see the flowers bloom?

4. Encourage the children to talk about times when their life hasn't been going well. Also ask them to describe when they've been happy. Be sensitive to particular children's situations.

5. Conclude that everyone has good days and bad days, good times and hard times. Remind them not to give up when things are tough because they usually get better.

**Variation:**  ✏ Explore what you can do when things aren't going well.

# MEMORY

**Visual memory skills will be reinforced as children become familiar with different expressions.**

*You will need:*  two copies of facial expressions from "Happy, Happy Me" activity
glue
scissors
posterboard cut in 4-inch squares

*Directions:*

1. Cut out the facial expressions and glue them to the posterboard squares. (Color them first if you wish.)

2. To introduce this game, spread out one set of the expressions; then let the children match the second set. Ask them to name the different expressions.

3. Mix up the cards. Then place them face down on the table or floor.

4. Ask one child at a time to turn over two cards. If the cards match, the child may keep them and have another turn. If they do not match, the next child may turn over two cards.

5. The game continues until all the cards have been matched.

*Variation:*

✏ Use fewer expressions for younger children. Make more expressions for older children.

# EXPRESSION HEADBANDS

These headbands will help children identify different feelings and will give them acceptable ways of dealing with their emotions.

**You will need:**   copy of facial expressions from "Happy, Happy Me"

six strips of 24″ × 2″ cardboard

glue

stapler

scissors

markers or crayons

**Directions:**

1. Color and cut out the facial expressions.

2. Make headbands from the cardboard strips by overlapping ends and stapling them to fit the children's heads.

3. Glue a different expression on each headband.

4. Pass out the headbands to six children and ask them to put them on.

5. Let one child at a time stand up while his or her classmates identify the expression. Tell them to make their face and body show that feeling. What might make a person feel that way? What can you do when you feel like that?

6. Have the children take turns wearing the headbands as they discuss what makes them feel that way.

**Variations:**

✏ Use the headbands as you sing "If You're Happy and You Know It."

✏ Let the children wear the headbands when they want to let others know how they are feeling.

# FACE THE DAY

This sign-in activity will encourage children to communicate how they are feeling.

***You will need:***   posterboard

one letter-size envelope for every two children

scissors, glue, markers

copies of expressions at the bottom of this page

***Directions:***

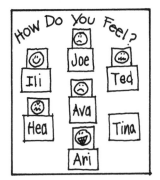

1. Write "How Do You Feel?" at the top of the posterboard.

2. Cut the envelopes in half. Glue them on the posterboard to create pockets; then write a child's name on each pocket.

3. Copy the expressions at the bottom of the page and cut them apart. Place them in a box or basket near the posterboard.

4. As children arrive at school each day, they can take an expression that represents how they feel and put it in their pocket.

Happy   Sleepy   Sad   Angry

# TROUBLE ROCK

The "trouble rock" gives children an outlet for talking about their problems and frustrations. In addition, it encourages them to think about what they can do to solve their own problems.

**You will need:**
rocks (let each child find their own rock on a nature walk; it should be about the size of their fist)

markers

wiggly eyes

yarn

scissors

glue

**Directions:**

1. Begin this activity by telling the children about a problem that you are dealing with in your life, or about a frustration you had when you were a child. Ask the children to share troubles that they have, too.

2. Let the children suggest what they do when they have a problem. Who do they talk to about it? Brainstorm ways to solve problems.

3. Explain that sometimes we have secrets or troubles that we might not be ready to talk to someone else about. A "trouble rock" is the perfect solution because it won't tell anyone else!

4. Have each child decorate his or her rock with markers, wiggly eyes, yarn hair, and so forth. Ask the children to think of a name for their rocks.

5. Encourage the children to take home their trouble rocks and tell them their secrets and concerns.

**Variations:**

✏ Suggest that children keep a diary or journal and write out their problems.

✏ Role-play how to solve various problems that the children might encounter, such as what to do about a bully on the bus, or how to save money for a new bicycle.

✏ Have the children write or draw pictures of their problems on a piece of paper. Then have them crumple them up and throw them in the trash.

# STRESS BOTTLES

Playing with these bottles and shaking them around will help children focus and calm down.

**You will need:**

plastic drink bottles with lids
white corn syrup
glitter
dish detergent
food coloring
vegetable oil
"super" glue

**Directions:**

1. Make several "stress bottles" following these directions.

   *Quiet Bottle* — Pour one-half cup of corn syrup into the bottle. Add several drops of food coloring. Glue on the lid; then gently move the bottle around to coat the sides as you quiet down.

   *Angry Bottle* — Pour one cup of water into the bottle. Add food coloring and a squirt of detergent. Glue on the lid; then shake, shake, shake out your anger.

   *Dream Bottle* — Put several tablespoons of glitter into the bottle. Add two drops of food coloring and then fill with water. Glue on the lid; then turn the bottle upside down and dream.

   *Relax Bottle* — Fill the bottle two-thirds full with water. Add several drops of food coloring; then fill it to the top with vegetable oil. Glue on the lid; then turn the bottle on its side and gently move it back and forth as you relax.

2. Give children the bottles to help them relieve stress, relax, or get rid of frustration.

**Variation:**

✏ If a child is very angry and out of control, take him or her outside and let the child "run" or "walk" it off.

**Hint:**

Supervise glitter carefully with young children, or substitute with crayon shavings.

137

# "LET IT ALL OUT" CENTER

This idea will give children an outlet for their anger and frustrations.

**You will need:**

pillow

play dough

old socks tied in knots

scrap paper

large basket or box

**Directions:**

1. Place the above items in the basket or box. Label it "Let It All Out."

2. Discuss things that make you angry. Ask the children to name things they can do when they get angry. Should you hit or hurt people when you're angry? Why not?

3. Show the children the different items in the basket and demonstrate how to use them to release anger. For example, punch the pillow, pinch the play dough, pull the knots out of the socks, or crumple the paper and throw it.

4. Place the baskets on a shelf or in a quiet corner of the classroom. Tell the children they are free to use any of the items in the box when they get angry.

5. When you sense a child becoming frustrated, redirect him or her to the "Let It All Out" Center.

**Variations:**

✏ Have the children draw pictures of things that make them angry. Put these together to make a book titled "I Get Angry When. . ."

✏ Role-play what to do when someone gets angry.

# SCRIBBLE PICTURE

Here's another technique children can use as an outlet for frustration and anger.

**You will need:**
large sheet of paper

crayons

**Directions:**

1. When the children are angry or upset, give them a large sheet of paper and a crayon. Tell them to scribble on the paper or draw a picture of what is making them upset.

2. Suggest if they still have some bad feelings to turn the paper over and scribble some more.

3. When they are finished, ask them if they would like to tell you about their picture. They can even crumple it up and throw it in the trash can if they would like.

4. Emphasize how much better we all feel when we let out bad feelings and don't keep them inside of us.

**Variations:**

✐ Tell the children to hold a crayon in each hand and scribble.

✐ Tape a large sheet of paper to a wall in the classroom to be used for a "graffiti" wall where children can draw pictures or scribble.

# RECORDING STUDIO

The recording studio gives children the opportunity to "air" their suggestions and vent their feelings. It also develops oral language skills.

***You will need:***

utility knife
tape recorder
blank tape
appliance box
paints and paintbrushes

***Directions:***

1. Cut out an opening or "door" on the front of the box.

2. Let the children decorate the outside of the box with paints, pictures, their names, or in any way they wish.

3. Make a sign that says "Recording Studio" to go on the box.

4. Tell the children that if they have something that's bothering them or something they are worried about, they can go to the recording studio and say it into the tape recorder. Explain that you will listen to it if they want you to, or it can be kept private.

***Variations:***

✎ If two children are having a conflict, suggest they go to the recording studio and work it out. Have each child tell his or her side of the story; then play back the tape for them to listen to so they can come up with a solution.

✎ Make a suggestion box for your classroom. Cut a slit in the top of a shoe box and attach a pencil and notepad. Try to respond to children's concerns with an explanation or seek their input on problems to let them know you really care.

***Hint:***

Be sure the children stay away from the utility knife.

# PICTURE TALKS

Children will develop perception and insight as they interpret feelings and human interactions in pictures and illustrations.

**You will need:** magazine pictures depicting different emotions such as happy, sad, surprised, scared, angry, and so on (include pictures that represent diversity)

construction paper or posterboard

glue

scissors

**Directions:**

1. Collect pictures of different feelings and mount them on construction paper or posterboard.

2. Show one picture at a time slowly to the children. "How do you think the people in the picture feel?" "Why?" "What do you think they are saying?"

3. Ask the children what they think happened before the picture was taken. What do they think happened after the picture was taken?

4. Continue showing pictures that reflect different feelings.

**Variations:**

✏ Have similar "picture talks" using books, paintings, and other media.

✏ Ask children to cut out their own magazine pictures and write or tell stories about how the people feel.

✏ Let children sort pictures according to the feelings reflected in them.

✏ Play different styles of music for the children, such as a lullaby, classical, jazz, folk, march, etc., and ask them to describe how the music makes them feel.

# WORD WEBBING

Children will be exposed to new vocabulary and will be encouraged to think divergently with webbing of feeling words.

**You will need:**  chalkboard and chalk OR large paper and markers

**Directions:**

1. Explain that there are many different words to describe how you are feeling. Begin with the word "sad" and ask the children to think of all the different words or things that make them feel sad.

2. Write the word "sad" on the chalkboard or paper. Then create a web around the word by writing what the children say.

3. Ask the children to read the words with you. Can they think of anything else?

4. Continue webbing with other feeling words.

**Variations:**

✏ Use magazine pictures of different emotions to create webs.

✏ Divide the children into small groups. Give each group a large sheet of paper. Write an emotion in the middle of the paper; then let them make their own word webs.

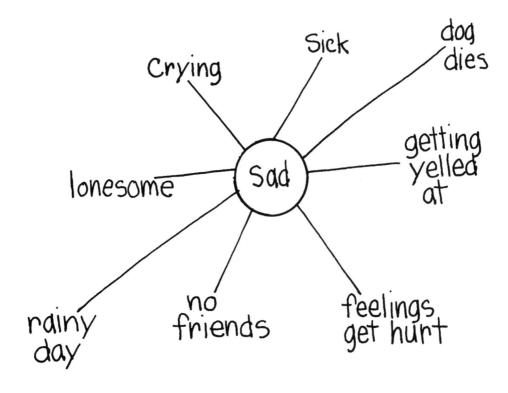

# GROUP CHART STORIES

Children will be encouraged to express their feelings, and they will be comforted in knowing that their peers also feel frightened, sad, proud, and angry at times. Additionally, language experience stories reinforce reading skills.

**You will need:**

chart paper
markers

**Directions:**

Happiness Is...
Al - Playing baseball
Ida - Eating pizza
Ron - Going to
.   the park
Louise - Watching
      T.V.
Tom - Running
Jan - Swinging

1. Gather the children in a small or large group and explain that sometimes you feel happy. Write the title "Happiness Is . . ." on the chart.

2. One at a time write each child's name. Then write what they say makes them happy. (Accept all responses and write exactly what the child says.)

3. Read the chart together. Or allow each child to individually read his or her sentence.

4. Let the children decorate the chart. Then hang it in the classroom.

**Variations:**

✐ Make language experience stories for other feelings such as "My Proudest Moment," "Things That Make My Temper Fly," "I Get the Shivers When . . .," or "My Most Embarrassing Moment."

✐ Write stories about what to do during a thunderstorm, when they have a nightmare, or other common situations when children might be frightened.

# WE CAN WORK IT OUT

By teaching these simple steps in problem solving, children will become empowered to work out their own conflicts. They will also learn that words are better than violence; by negotiating, everyone can feel good.

**You will need:**   posterboard or large tablet

markers

**Directions:**

1. Print the following steps in conflict resolution on the poster or tablet:

> ### WORKING IT OUT
> 1. Stay cool.
> 2. Let everyone tell his or her side of the story.
> 3. What is the problem?
> 4. Think of ways to solve the problem.
> 5. Decide on the best solution.
> 6. Do it!

2. Call a class meeting and review some of the conflicts children commonly have in the classroom. Let children share ways they try to work out their own problems.

3. Review the steps for conflict resolution on the poster. Tell the children that you will hang it in the room so they can refer to it when they have a disagreement.

4. Role-play various situations using the steps on the chart.

5. As the need arises, act as a mediator to help children work through the process.

6. Be *consistent*! (This takes a great deal of time and patience, but the results will be well worth the effort.)

**Variations:**

✎  Create a special place in the classroom called the "peace place" where children can go to resolve conflicts.

✎  Let children take turns being the mediator when there is a conflict.

# SUGGESTION CIRCLE

The suggestion circle provides children with a tool for solving their dilemmas and promotes creative problem solving.

**You will need:**   no materials are needed

**Directions:**

1. Have 8 to 10 children stand or sit in a circle.

2. Ask each child to think of a problem he or she has. It might be at school, at home, or in the neighborhood.

3. Explain that in a "suggestion circle," one person at a time describes his or her problem to the rest of the group. Everyone has a few minutes to think of a "suggestion" for that problem. Go around the circle and let each person offer a solution to the problem. All the person with the problem may say is, "Thank You." ("It won't work" or "I've already tried that" are not allowed.)

4. Let the children volunteer to share their problems and then listen to their peers' suggestions.

5. Bring closure to the activity by emphasizing that there are many different ways to handle problems, and that we must be willing to try new things.

**Variation:**

✎ Bring classroom problems to the suggestion circle. You state what the concern is; then children offer solutions to the problem. (It might be fighting, running in the hall, taking materials that belong to others, etc.)

# BOOBOO BEAR

Children will develop empathy for others as they explore ways to comfort the toy bear.

*You will need:*  toy bear (or other stuffed animal)

box of bandaids

*Directions:*

1. Put a bandaid on the bear ahead of time.

2. At group time, bring out Booboo Bear and tell the children he is very sad because he got hurt. Ask the children how they think he got hurt. (Accept all answers.)

3. "How could you make Booboo Bear feel better?" Let the children role-play what they would do to comfort him.

4. Give each child in the room a bandaid. Tell them to unwrap it and put it somewhere on their body.

5. Let the children take turns making up stories about how they got their booboo. Have classmates demonstrate how they would take care of their friend.

*Variations:*

- Discuss the different reasons people cry and how to comfort them.

- Let the children draw pictures of what makes them cry. Put their pages together to make a "Sad Book."

# SNUGGLES AND STONES

**Children will become aware of how their actions impact upon others. With this activity, they will be encouraged to be kind to friends.**

***You will need:***

one ziplock baggie for each child

rocks

cotton balls

***Directions:***

1. Give each child a ziplock bag. Go out on the playground and ask the children to find five small stones to put in their baggies.

2. Return to the classroom and give each child five cotton balls to also go in their baggies.

3. Discuss how you feel when someone smiles at you or says something nice to you. It makes you feel warm and "snuggly." However, when people hurt you or say something unkind to you, it makes you feel bad.

4. Explain that the cotton balls are like the good, snuggly feelings, but the stones are those bad, cold feelings. Tell the children that whenever someone gives them a good feeling, they should let them know by giving them a cotton ball. (Let the children give you examples of what they might do to receive a cotton ball, such as help a friend, say something nice to them, or share a game.) On the other hand, if someone hits them, takes a toy away, or hurts their feelings, they should give them a stone to let them know they don't like it.

5. After the children have had several hours to give away their stones and cotton balls, call them together and review the activity. How did they feel when they received a stone? How did they feel when they received a cotton ball? If you want other people to feel good and to like you, how do you need to treat them?

***Variation:***

✏ Simplify the activity by just giving each child one or two cotton balls and stones.

# "I WISH" WAND

The "wish wand" allows children to verbalize their fantasies and to share their dreams with others.

**You will need:**   cardboard tube from a pants hanger (a stick or wooden dowel can also be used)

glue, glitter

feather, tinsel, ribbon, or other decorations

**Directions:**

1. Dip one end of the cardboard tube in glue; then roll it in glitter and allow to dry.

2. Add a feather, tinsel, or other decorations.

3. Wave the wand over the children and ask them what they would wish for if they found a magic wand.

4. Pass the wand around and let each child make a wish. Encourage children to expand on their wishes by asking, "Why?"

**Variations:**

- Write the children's wishes on a language experience chart.

- Let the children make their own wands by dipping the end of a wooden chopstick in glue and then sprinkling it with glitter.

- Take a plastic bottle and put several tablespoons of iridescent glitter in the bottom. Fill it with water; then glue on the top. Have the children shake the bottle and make a wish.

> ☆ Make a Wish ☆
> Andy- I wish I'd win the lottery.
> Bonita- I wish I had a baby brother.
> Ian- I wish I could hit a home run.
> Danielle- I wish I could be a singer.

**Hint:**   Supervise glitter carefully with young children.

148

# WANTS AND NEEDS

Children are often jealous or resentful because they cannot have the toys or clothes that their friends have or they see on television. This activity will help them discriminate the difference between things they want and things they truly need.

***You will need:***
apple

toy

chalkboard or chart paper

paper

magazines, newspapers

scissors

crayons

glue

***Directions:***

1. Show the children the apple and the toy. "Which one of these things do we really need to live, and which one would just be nice to have?" Explain that some things we really need, like clothing, food, and shelter. Other objects are simply things we want, like toys and video games; we don't really need them.

2. Write "wants" and "needs" on the chalkboard and draw a line between them. Have the children give you examples of each and write them on the board.

3. Give each child a piece of paper and ask them to fold it in half. On one side write "wants" and on the other side write "needs." Let the children cut out magazine pictures or draw pictures of objects they want and need.

***Variation:***

✏ Have the children brainstorm what they can do if there is something they "want" that their family cannot afford.

# A RIDE IN THE SKY

This activity will help children relax and calm down. It will also give them the opportunity to dream and escape.

*You will need:*  soft music

*Directions:*
1. Turn off the lights in the classroom and ask the children to find a comfortable place to sit or lie down.

2. Ask them to close their eyes as you begin playing the music.

3. Tell the children that you are going to take them on a ride in the sky. Have them pretend to climb onto a cloud. "See the blue sky and feel the cool breeze all around you. Ride your cloud to a place where you can be happy."

4. After 5 to 10 minutes, explain that it is time to ride their clouds back to school. Turn off the music and have the children gently wake up as they stretch their arms and legs.

5. Ask children to describe where they went on their clouds and how they felt.

*Variations:*
- Give children paper and crayons so they can draw pictures of their ride in the sky.

- Ride an imaginary pony, bird, rocket ship, or magic carpet to "dream land."

# ME MASSAGE

This is a simple relaxation technique children can use to relieve stress at school or home.

**You will need:**

nonallergenic body lotion
soft music

**Directions:**

1. Ask each child to find his or her own space on the floor where he or she can sit or stretch out comfortably.

2. Squirt some lotion in each child's hands.

3. Turn off the lights and begin playing the soft music.

4. Demonstrate as you slowly talk through the following steps:

   a. Rub your hands together.

   b. Gently squeeze and pull up on the left hand.

   c. Squeeze and pull up on the right hand.

   d. Slowly pull at each finger on the right hand; then the left hand.

   e. Rub up and down on the right arm; then stretch it.

   f. Rub up and down on the left arm; then stretch it.

   g. Close your eyes and breath in 2 – 3 – 4; then out 2 – 3 – 4.

5. Conclude by having the children describe how they feel. Suggest they try this activity at home when they get upset.

**Variation:**

✏ Try a body massage when the class is rowdy or on a rainy day.

# FLOPPY AND STIFF

These are some other techniques that will give children an outlet for their stress.

***You will need:*** no materials are needed

***Directions:***

1. Gather the children and ask them if they ever feel like they're going to explode. Do they ever feel really nervous and upset? Let the children share what they do when they get nervous.

2. Demonstrate how to do the following exercises to get rid of bad feelings and to relax.

### FLOPPY AND STIFF

Tell the children to stand up and then flop over from the waist like a rag doll. Show them how to wiggle their arms and relax. When you say "Staff," they should stand up straight and make their body as stiff as they can. Have them tense up and be tight for 10 to 15 seconds; then say "Floppy," as they bend over and relax again. Continue saying "Floppy" and "Stiff" every 15 seconds.

### BALLOONS

Ask the children to get in a very small ball shape on the floor. Tell them to pretend that they are a balloon and to slowly fill themselves up with air . . . bigger and bigger until they are standing with arms outstretched, feet apart, and cheeks full of air. Now have them slowly let all the air out as they exhale and return to a small ball on the floor. Continue inhaling and blowing up like a balloon and then slowly exhaling.

### SLOW BREATHING

Teach the children how to breathe slowly in and then let the air out as they count to ten. Practice saying "I am" slowly as they inhale and "wonderful" as they slowly exhale.

# ALONE ZONE

Children often need a quiet place where they can "escape" to get themselves together, relax, or find some peace. It is particularly important to provide children with this space in a busy classroom.

**You will need:**

appliance box

utility knife

paints and paintbrushes (or markers)

pillows

**Directions:**

1. Ask the children what they do when they want to be alone. Suggest making a special place in the classroom where children can relax and be by themselves.

2. Cut a door and several windows out of the appliance box. (An adult will need to do this.)

3. Let the children decorate the box with paints or markers. These are some suggestions:

### BEAR CAVE

(Paint brown and fill with teddy bears.)

### DREAM CENTER

(Hang glitter stars and cotton clouds on the inside.)

### QUIET GARDEN

(Decorate with flowers and cover with an old lace tablecloth or curtain.)

4. Place the box in a quiet corner of the classroom and fill with pillows and books. (Limit the alone zone to one or two children at a time.)

**Variation:**

✏ Add a tape player with soft music.

**Hint:**

Be sure the children stay away from the utility knife.

153

# ALONE AND WITH A FRIEND

*You will need:*    chalkboard and chalk

paper and crayons

*Directions:*

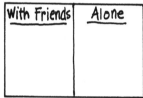

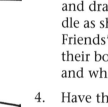

1. Discuss activities that you like to do with friends. Ask the children if they ever just want to be alone.

2. On one side of the chalkboard write "With Friends" and on the other side write "Alone." Have the children name things they like to do alone and with a group as you write them on the board.

3. Give each child a sheet of paper. Demonstrate how to fold it in half and draw a line down the middle crease. Fold in one side to the middle as shown; then fold in the other side. On the left side write "With Friends" and on the right side print "Alone." Tell the children to open their book and draw what they like to do with friends on the left side and what they like to do alone on the right.

4. Have the children suggest what they can say when they choose to be alone. Where can they go to be alone? What can they do if they want someone to play with them?

*Variations:*

✎  Let the children make a large mural of activities they like to do alone and with friends using paints, crayons, or markers.

✎  Have each child contribute a page to a class book entitled "Fun Things to Do When You're Alone."

# DO NOT DISTURB

Children, like adults, have times when they need to be alone. This door hanger will give them a tool for reflecting that need.

**You will need:**
heavy paper
door hanger pattern on the following page
scissors
markers, crayons, or collage materials

**Directions:**

1. Prepare a "Do Not Disturb" sign ahead of time. Show it to the children and explain that hotels have signs like this that people can hang outside their door when they want to be alone.

2. Let the children trace around the door hanger pattern. Then cut it out.

3. Give the children crayons, markers, or collage materials to decorate their door hangers.

**Variations:**

- How many different ways can you say "I want to be alone?"

- Let the children decorate door hangers with their initials, magazine pictures, or things they like.

- On the reverse side of "Do Not Disturb," have children write "I feel good. Come on in."

# DOOR HANGER PATTERN

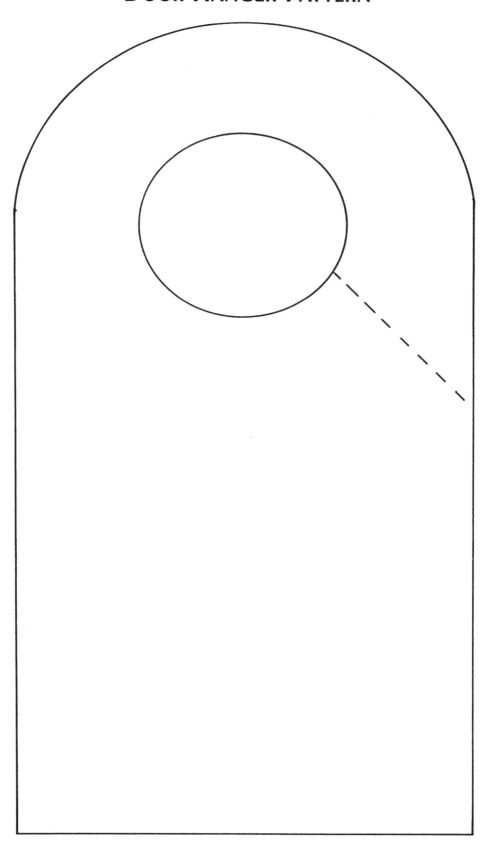

# "ME" BAGS

This project will provide children with a concrete way of sharing how they think they appear to others, and what they are really like on the inside.

**You will need:**
box with a lid
small toy
one lunch bag for each child
old magazines
scissors
glue
markers or crayons

**Directions:**

1. Hide the toy in the box. Ask the children to guess what is inside the box. Can they tell for sure what's inside the box by looking at the outside?

2. Relate the box to people. Sometimes we appear one way on the outside, but we are different inside.

3. Give each child a lunch bag and the magazines and art supplies. Have them decorate the outside of the bag with magazine pictures and words that describe how they appear to others. Tell them to cut out pictures of what they are like on the inside and put them in the bag.

4. Give the children an opportunity to share their bags with classmates. To conclude, ask children if they learned anything new about a friend.

**Variations:**

✉ Large paper grocery bags can also be used for this project.

✉ To simplify the project, give each child an envelope. Ask the children to glue a picture of what they're like on the outside on the front of the envelope, and to put a picture that represents them on the inside in the envelope.

# MASKS

Mask-making will give children an opportunity to express their inner feelings, be creative, and verbalize what causes different emotions.

**You will need:**
9″ × 12″ construction paper
safety scissors, stapler, glue
markers, crayons
scrap paper
yarn, feathers, and other collage materials

**Directions:**

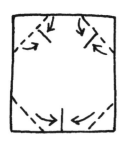

1. Trim off the four corners on the paper as shown.

2. Cut 2-inch slits along the top corners. Cut one 2-inch slit up the bottom edge.

3. Fold over slits on the top and staple to make the forehead. Fold over bottom slits to make the chin.

4. Hold the mask to the face and mark where the eyes, nose, and mouth will be. Cut small openings for these features.

5. Let the children describe different feelings. Ask them to decorate their mask to reflect one of those feelings. Provide them with crayons, markers, scrap paper, and collage materials.

6. When children are finished, let them take turns putting on their masks while their friends guess the emotion.

**Variations:**

✏ Does the way your face look always reflect the way you're feeling inside?

✏ Have the children go to the library and find out how masks are used in different cultures.

✏ Use the masks to make a bulletin board.

✏ Tell the children to cover their faces with their hands and pretend to put on a "happy" mask. Talk about what makes them happy. Next, have them cover their face again and put on an "angry" mask. Continue having the children put on different masks and discuss what makes them feel that way.

# DEAR DIARY

Writing skills will be practiced as children learn an effective way to express their thoughts and feelings.

**You will need:**

two sheets of 4-1/4″ × 6″ posterboard for each child

11″ × 14″ fabric scraps

ten sheets of 8 1/2″ × 11″ paper for each child

scissors

glue

two sheets of 4″ × 5″ construction paper for each child

needle and thread or sewing machine

**Directions:**

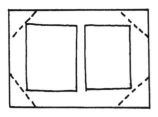

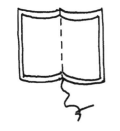

1. Have the children glue the posterboard to the inside of the fabric as shown. (Leave 1/4 inch between the posterboards.)

2. Trim the corners. Then fold over the edges of the fabric and glue to the posterboard.

3. Glue construction paper onto the fabric edges to finish the inside.

4. Fold the paper in half and match with the fold in the center of the book. Sew in place with a needle and thread or stitch on a sewing machine.

5. Set aside a time each day for the children to write in their "diaries." Encourage them to write about their feelings, problems, fears, friendships, exciting events, and so forth.

**Variations:**

✏ Provide time for children to share their journals—if they wish—with their classmates.

✏ Be available to offer the children advice with concerns they write about in their journals.

**Hint:**

All sewing (whether by hand or by machine) should be done by an adult.

# MAKING FACES

Children will gain insight into identifying different feelings.

**You will need:**    pictures of different expressions (cut these from magazines or enlarge the illustrations from the activity "Happy, Happy Me")

**Directions:**

1.  Divide the children into pairs and explain that they are going to "make faces" at each other.

2.  Hold up one of the expressions for the children to see. Now tell them to make that same face at their partner. Extend the activity by asking them to talk about what makes them feel that way.

3.  Continue holding up the different expressions as the children make similar faces at their partner and discuss those emotions.

4.  Conclude by having the children make silly faces at each other as they try to make their partners laugh.

**Variation:**    ✏ Describe different situations. Then have the children make how their face would look. Do people always feel the same way about situations?

# FEELINGS CHARADES

Playing a game of charades about feelings will help children identify various emotions and become more perceptive of body language.

**You will need:**

copy of the following page
box or basket

**Directions:**

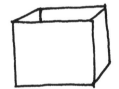

1. Cut along the dotted lines of the situations on the following page and place them in a box or basket.

2. Explain that in the game of charades you cannot use your voice, but must communicate with your face and body motions. Pantomime several examples, such as eating an ice cream cone, batting a ball, or putting on your shoes.

3. Let one child at a time draw a situation from the basket. Ask that child to act out what it says as classmates try to guess. Encourage the children to identify how they would feel in a similar situation.

4. The first person to guess correctly draws the next situation.

**Variations:**

- Divide the children into teams to play this game.

- Have children act out situations with a partner or small group.

- Let younger children use words to act out the scenes.

# Charades

| | |
|---|---|
| You are lost in a big store. | Someone calls you a name and hurts your feelings. |
| Your best friend moves away. | You win a new bicycle in a contest. |
| It's your birthday and you have a big party. | Your dog runs away. |
| You lose your homework. | You receive a special award at school. |
| Your mother yells at you for not cleaning your room. | You get sick and miss a big ball game. |
| It's the day before you're going on vacation with your family. | Everyone gets invited to a party but you. |
| It's a beautiful day, but you can't find anyone at home to play with you. | Someone takes your pencil without asking. |
| You're in a play at school and you forget your lines. | You get "100" on a test. |
| You smell your favorite dinner cooking when you get home from school. | No one chooses you to be on their team at P.E. |
| You make the winning point in a game. | You drop your lunch tray in the middle of the cafeteria. |
| You fall down and hurt your knee. | You see a fire truck going down the street where you live. |

# FACE CHANGE

As children create various facial expressions, they will become familiar with different feelings and emotions.

**You will need:**

felt (body colors)

red, white, & black felt scraps

scissors

patterns on following two pages

**Directions:**

1. Use the patterns on the following two pages to cut out several heads and facial features.

2. Give the children the heads and let them experiment with creating different facial expressions.

3. Ask them to make a happy face. Encourage them to tell you what makes them happy.

4. Continue by having them make angry, surprised, sleepy, scared, or sad faces. Discuss what causes them to feel that way.

**Variations:**

- Make faces and features out of construction paper. Laminate; then attach with Velcro®.

- Divide children into pairs. Let one child make a face. Then let the other child make up a story about why the face feels that way.

- Make copies of the features for each child. Let the children glue them on a paper plate to create different expressions.

- Children can also use play dough to create different expressions.

- To make a flannel board, glue felt to the inside lid of a pizza box. Store features in the box. Then use the flannel board and facial features to create stories.

# FACE MAKER

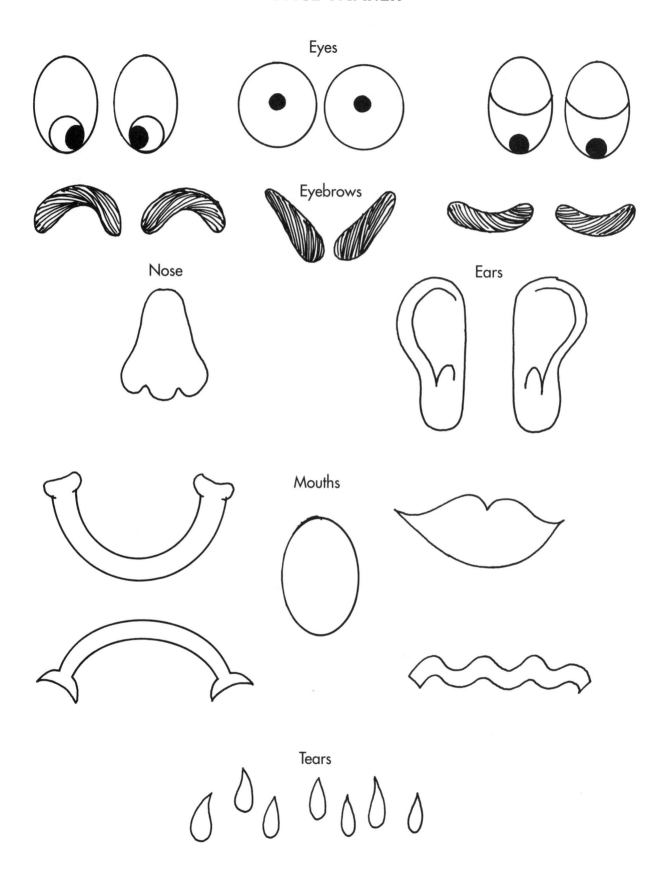

# FACE

Hair
(Enlarge to fit head.)

# FEELING FACE SANDWICHES

Creating a sandwich with a facial expression is another way children can identify their emotions and verbalize their feelings.

*You will need:*     paper plates, plastic knives, napkins
circle cookie cutter
bread
peanut butter
raisins
O-shaped cereal
shredded carrots

*Directions:*
1. Wash your hands.

2. Give each child a piece of bread and have them cut out a circle shape with the cookie cutter. (Save the crusts for the birds.)

3. Spread peanut butter on the bread.

4. Ask the children how they are feeling. Give them raisins, O-shaped cereal, and shredded carrots to make a sandwich that shows how they are feeling.

5. Encourage the children to describe their feelings to their friends as they eat their sandwiches.

*Variations:*
✏ Bean sprouts, cheese, nuts, and other toppings can also be used to decorate the sandwiches.

✏ Mix milk with food coloring. Let children paint this on a piece of bread with a cotton swab to make a facial expression. Toast and eat.

# IF YOU'RE HAPPY

Change the words of this familiar song to incorporate different feelings.

**You will need:**  no materials are needed

**Directions:**

1. Sing the first verse of "If You're Happy":

   If you're happy and you know it clap your hands.
   (*Clap, clap.*)

   If you're happy and you know it clap your hands.
   (*Clap, clap.*)

   If you're happy and you know it,
   then your face will surely show it.

   If you're happy and you know it clap your hands.
   (*Clap, clap.*)

2. Ask the children if everyone is happy all the time. Teach them the verses below for when they have other feelings:

   If you're sad and you know it rub your eyes. . .
   (*Pretend to cry as you rub your eyes.*)

   If you're mad and you know it stomp your feet. . .
   (*Stomp feet.*)

   If you're scared and you know it shiver and shake. . .
   (*Shake all over.*)

   If you're surprised and you know it say, "Oh, my!. . .
   (*Put hands in air as you say, "Oh, my."*)

   If you're sleepy and you know it give a yawn. . .
   (*Stretch arms and pretend to yawn.*)

**Variations:**

✏ Let the children make up their own verses and motions to this song.

✏ Write the words "happy," "sad," "mad," "scared," "surprised," and "sleepy" on flash cards. Then hold them up as everyone sings the different verses.

# MY FEELING BOOK

"My Feeling Book" fosters reading and writing skills, as well as the acceptance of feelings.

**You will need:**  one copy each of the following two pages for each child
stapler
scissors
markers or crayons (body colors)

**Directions:**

1.  Have the children cut along the dotted lines of the "feeling book" on the following two pages and staple the pages together.

2.  Read the book together, encouraging the children to talk about what makes them feel that way. Ask them to suggest different ways to handle those feelings.

3.  Let the children draw their own facial expressions for the different emotions.

**Variations:**

✏ Have older children write a sentence to go with each feeling in the book.

✏ Talk about how adults have different feelings, too. How can they help their parents if they are sad, angry, or scared?

# MY FEELING BOOK

Sometimes I'm happy, and that's okay.

BY _____

---

Sometimes I'm sad, and that's okay.

Sometimes I'm angry, and that's okay.

Sometimes I'm afraid, and that's okay.

Sometimes I'm proud, and that's okay.

Sometimes I'm shy, and that's okay.

Sometimes I'm sleepy, and that's okay.

GOOD NIGHT!

# REFLECTIONS

A closing activity before the children go home each day will help them focus on positive things that happened in school. They will leave with good feelings.

**You will need:**   no materials are needed

**Directions:**

1. Gather the children before they go home and help them review their day in sequential order.

2. Ask questions similar to the ones below:

   "What did you do today that made you feel proud?"

   "What did you do today to be a good friend?"

   "What mistake did you make that you will do differently next time?"

   "What did you do today that you enjoyed?"

3. Tell the children something special that they will be doing at school the next day so they will look forward to it.

4. Close with the song "It Is Time to Say Good-Bye" (*Tune:* "Coming 'Round the Mountain"):

   It is time to say good-bye to all our friends.
   It is time to say good-bye to all our friends.
   It is time to say good-bye.
   Give a smile and wink your eye.
   It is time to say good-bye to all your friends.

   (*Clap your hands and stomp your feet as you sing.
   Then end by waving good-bye.*)

**Variations:**

Monday, May 14
Today we learned a new song about alligators.
We made stick puppets.
Joey had a birthday.

✏ Whisper a positive comment in each child's ear before he or she leaves for the day.

✏ Have children turn to a friend sitting near them and talk about their school day.

✏ Make a language experience chart of daily reflections.

✏ Let one child draw a picture of something special that happens each day. Date the pictures; then make a class book with them.

171

# 4

# Same and Different

Children who grow up in an environment that is bias-free are much more likely to be accepting of the differences in themselves and others. This section is a resource of games, crafts, music, and meaningful activities that celebrates the likenesses and differences in all of us.

# THUMBPRINT DETECTIVES

Children will explore how unique and special they are from their own thumbprints. They'll also develop visual discrimination and visual memory skills from this activity.

*You will need:*

ink pad
3″ × 5″ index cards or heavy white paper
magnifying glass
pencils

*Directions:*

1. Have the children hold up their thumbs and look at them carefully. Explain that everyone in the world has his or her own unique fingerprint and that detectives can often identify a person just by his or her fingerprint.

2. Demonstrate how to make a thumbprint by pressing the thumb on the ink pad and applying it to paper.

3. Ask the children to write their name on one side of the index card; then turn it over and put their thumbprint on the other side. Let them look at their prints with a magnifying glass and compare their lines with those of friends.

4. Mix the cards up. Challenge the children to pick out their print from all the others.

5. Discuss what else makes the children unique and special.

*Variations:*

✆ Make footprints, elbow prints, and prints of other body parts and compare.

✆ Invite local police officers to your school to make identification cards with the children's fingerprints.

✆ Let the children make thumbprint creatures by adding details to the thumbprints with fine-tip markers or colored pencils. They can make flowers, insects, people, or animals.

# INSIDE, OUTSIDE

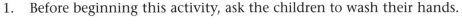

With this activity children will explore how people are different on the outside, but very much the same on the inside.

**You will need:**
different types of apples (red, yellow, green)

knife

napkins

**Directions:**

1. Before beginning this activity, ask the children to wash their hands.

2. Display the apples and pass one of each around the room for the children to examine. Discuss how the apples are alike. How are they different?

3. Take a red apple and ask the children what they think is inside it. Cut the apple in half diagonally and show them the "star." Cut the yellow and green apples in half. How are the apples alike inside?

4. Conclude by reminding the children how people are like the apples. We are different on the outside, but there's a "star" or something special about each one of us on the inside.

5. Eat the apples for snack!

**Variations:**

✆ Cut the apples into eighths and let the children sample each variety. Do they taste the same? Vote to see which is their favorite.

✆ Make apple prints by dipping the apple halves in paint and applying them to paper. Can you see a star?

✆ Do a similar activity using a brown egg and a white egg. How are they different on the outside, but the same on the inside?

**Hint:**
Be sure the children stay away from the knife.

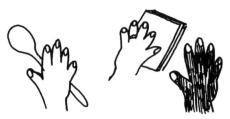

# HANDS THAT HELP

As children visit the different helpers in the school, they will discover that although our hands are very much alike, we all have different skills and jobs we can do.

**You will need:**   no materials are needed

**Directions:**
1. Invite the children to go on a "field trip" with you around your school.

2. As you visit the secretary, cafeteria workers, principal, custodian, librarian, and other school helpers, ask them to show their hands to the children. Then let them describe what their hands do to help the children in the school.

3. On returning to the classroom, ask the children how everyone's hands were alike. How were they different? What would happen if they didn't have the different helpers in the school?

4. Have the children look at their own hands; then compare them with their friends' hands. Encourage the children to tell a special job their hands can do to help.

**Variation:**   ✏ Ask the children to write thank-you notes or draw pictures for the different school helpers.

# HAGALENA MAGALENA

"Hagalena Magalena" is a silly song that emphasizes the importance of what is inside us, rather than outward appearances.

**You will need:**   no materials are needed

**Directions:**

1. Explain that you have a new song to teach the children about a unique lady named Hagalena Magalena.

   *"Hagalena Magalena"* (*Tune:* "Shortnin' Bread")

   *Chorus:*   Hagalena Magalena Oopsadina Walkadina
   Hoca Poca Loca was her name.

   Her head was shaped like a baseball bat,
   And right on top was a funny old hat.
   (*Chorus.*)

   She had two hairs on her head.
   One was alive and the other was dead.
   (*Chorus.*)

   She had two eyes in her head.
   One was purple and the other was red.
   (*Chorus.*)

   She had two teeth in her mouth.
   One pointed north and the other pointed south.
   (*Chorus.*)

   Her hips were like two battleships.
   One stayed in port while the other took trips.
   (*Chorus.*)

   Her feet were as flat as a bathroom mat.
   How did they ever get like that?
   (*Chorus.*)

   She had a heart, so I'm told,
   That was made of purest gold.
   (*Chorus.*)

2. Discuss what it means to have a "heart of gold." Did it really matter what Hagalena Magalena looked like on the outside? Ask the children to share ways they can act so others will say they have a "heart of gold."

**Variation:**   ✏ Have the children draw or paint pictures of Hagalena Magalena. Put them together to make a class book.

177

# AROUND THE ROOM WITH MULTICULTURAL IDEAS

The multicultural curriculum is one that represents people of all ethnic groups, ages, sexes, and abilities in meaningful ways. The following are exciting ideas for implementing the multicultural curriculum in learning centers.

***Directions:***

1.  *Dramatic Play* — In the Dramatic Play area place food containers and utensils for different ethnic foods. Provide the children with multi-ethnic dolls, as well as clothes, shoes, hats, and jewelry from a variety of cultures.

2.  *Library* — Include folk tales from different cultures, books representative of all areas of our society, and printed materials in different languages.

3.  *Manipulatives* — Make nonsexist puzzles, graduated stacking dolls from another culture, and coins and beads from other countries available to children.

4.  *Art* — Offer children crayons, markers, paint, and clay in various body colors. Display pictures of art from different areas of the world, and let the children experiment with art media of other cultures (rice paper, shells, origami paper, fabrics, etc.).

5.  *Cooking* — Help children prepare ethnic foods for snack time. Include ethnic meals on the monthly menu.

6.  *Music* — Play tapes and songs from around the world. Let the children experiment with ethnic instruments. Teach them a song in a foreign language.

# AROUND THE ROOM WITH MULTICULTURAL IDEAS
## *(Continued)*

7. *Blocks* — Put up pictures of different kinds of homes (mobile, apartments, single-family dwellings, rural, suburban, homes from other countries) in the Block area. Add multiethnic figures, different types of transportation, and a variety of building materials (straw, sticks, canvas, etc.) for the children to construct with.

8. *Sensory* — Give the children animals from different habitats (arctic, rainforest, desert, forest) to play with in sand and water. Freeze water in plastic containers to create icebergs for play with the arctic animals.

9. *Math* — Make graphs that compare families. Use manipulatives from other cultures for sorting, counting, and making sets.

10. *Photos* — Display photos of different kinds of families and different ethnic groups. Include photos that reflect the diversity in our society; men and women in different careers, older adults, and children with varying abilities. Also display photos of the children in the room with their own families.

11. *Globes and Maps* — Provide children with globes and maps so they can identify different countries as they are discussed.

# BILINGUAL BOOKS

These books provide an excellent opportunity to introduce children to different languages.

***You will need:***

paper lunch bags
scissors
glue
brad fasteners or stapler
old school supply catalogs
markers

***Directions:***

1.  Take 5 to 6 lunch bags and attach the openings together with brad fasteners or staples to make a book.

2.  Glue a common classroom object or toy you have cut from the catalog on the left-hand side of each sack.

3.  Fold over the bottom section on each sack. On the top write the name for the object in English. Open the flap and write the word for the object in another language.

4.  Read the book to the children. Then let them take turns reading it.

***Variations:***

✏ This is a wonderful way to include children who speak a language other than English.

✏ Have children make their own bilingual books. Involve parents in this project.

# READING AND SINGING AROUND THE WORLD

Children will become aware of different languages and forms of writing and music with this discovery project.

**You will need:**
newspapers, magazines, or books written in different languages
foreign language tapes
music tapes from other cultures
tape recorder
globe or world map
paper and pencils

**Directions:**

1.  Ask parents and children to be explorers and look for printed material from other countries. Also ask them to share tapes of music from other cultures. (Libraries, embassies, and bookstores are other good sources.)

2.  Set up a display area in your classroom for children to investigate the printed materials and listen to the tapes. Add a globe or world map and help them identify countries where various languages are spoken.

3.  Compare the English alphabet with other alphabets. Demonstrate how different cultures read from the bottom to the top of the page or from right to left.

4.  Add paper and pencils for the children to try to write using different alphabets.

**Variations:**

✏ Make bilingual labels for your classroom.

✏ Encourage children who speak a second language to "teach" it to you and their classmates.

✏ Learn how to say "please" and "thank you" and other common phrases in different languages.

# LET'S GO SHOPPING

A visit to a grocery store will quickly expand children's knowledge of many products that come from around the world.

**You will need:**
grocery store
shopping list
pencil

**Directions:**

1.  Arrange a field trip to a grocery store in your community.

2.  As you go around the store, challenge the children to find products from other countries.

3.  Make a list of all the foods and where they are imported from.

4.  Buy fruits from other countries. Then have a tasting party back at school.

**Variations:**

✏ Ask the children to look around their homes for toys and clothes that were made in foreign countries. Have the children write a list of these items.

✏ Divide older children into groups and have a scavenger hunt in the grocery store. Give them a list similar to the one below:

---

Find a product that comes from Hawaii.

What is a fruit from South America?

Name a product from Greece.

Find two foods from Europe.

Name three foods from the ocean.

How many other imported foods can you find?

---

# A WORLD OF BREAD

Similarities and differences in breads served around the world will be explored with this "delicious" project.

**You will need:**
bagels (Austria)
croissants (France)
tortillas (Mexico)
pita (Middle East)
matzoh (Israel)
pumpernickel (Germany)
cornbread (Southern U.S.)
plates, napkins

**Directions:**

1. Cut the above breads into bite-size pieces, and have the children wash their hands before you begin.

2. Ask the children what their favorite type of bread is. How many different types of bread can they name?

3. Explain that people in different parts of the world eat different kinds of bread. Show each sample and tell them about the country with which the bread is associated.

4. Encourage the children to sample each kind of bread. Which one is their favorite?

**Variations:**

✏ Make a graph of the children's favorite bread.

✏ Show the children on the globe the countries where the different types of bread are eaten.

✏ Sample fruit, rice dishes, or sweets from different cultures.

✏ Demonstrate cooking utensils used in different cultures.

✏ Let the children make homemade biscuits or other quick breads.

# WHAT'S COOKING AT YOUR HOUSE?

Families will enjoy sharing their favorite recipes, and children will have the opportunity to taste many new foods.

**You will need:**   one copy of the following letter for each child
napkins, plates, silverware
construction paper
copy paper
crayons
stapler

**Directions:**

1. Send home a copy of the attached letter several weeks before your international feast.

2. Remind the children several days before the event and build it up.

3. On the day of the feast, let each child talk about his or her dish. Encourage the children to try a little of all the different foods.

4. Talk about how the different foods taste. Which ones are sweet? Spicy? Crunchy?

5. Make copies of all the recipes and give one set to each child. Staple them in the construction paper to make a recipe book, and let the children decorate the covers with crayons.

**Variations:**

✏ Invite the families to class for an international potluck dinner.

✏ Point out on a globe or world map where the foods originated from.

# WE'RE HAVING AN INTERNATIONAL FEAST!

Dear parents:

On _____ we will have an international feast. We are asking each family to send in a favorite dish from their native country or ethnic group.

We would also like you to send in a copy of the recipe. If there is a special story behind it, we'd appreciate your including that, too. We will then reproduce all of these recipes and make a cookbook for each child. That way you will be able to try out some of the different dishes at your home.

Please involve your child in the preparation of the recipe. Send the dish in on the day of the feast in a plastic bag or box with your name on it. Let us know if it needs to be heated or refrigerated.

The children will be excited about sharing their special family food with their friends, and they will have "yummy" fun learning to try new foods.

Thanks for your support.

Sincerely,

_____

P.S. On your recipe please include:

Child's
Name _____

Name of
Recipe _____

Native
Origin _____

# WHAT ARE YOU WEARING?

As children try on clothes, shoes, and accessories from other countries, they will develop more accepting attitudes toward different modes of dress.

**You will need:**

clothes, shoes, hats, jewelry, and other accessories from different cultures
full-length mirror

**Directions:**

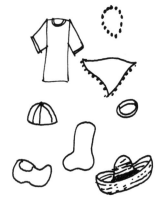

1. Begin collecting hats, shoes, clothes, etc., from different cultures. (Ask parents to donate items to your classroom.)

2. Place the objects in the Dramatic Play area for free exploration. Make sure children have a mirror so they can look at themselves!

3. Choose one child to put on the clothing from a particular culture and model it for the class. Explain what country the dress originated in. How is the clothing suited to the climate in that country?

**Variations:**

- Take photos of the children modeling the different clothing. Display the photos with labels.

- Display pictures of people with their native dress. Ask the children if they think they wear the clothes every day. On what special occasions might they wear those clothes?

- Encourage parents from other cultures to wear their native dress to your class and explain the different items to the children.

# FAMILY CULTURE BOX

**You will need:**   one box with a lid for each child

postcards, books, clothes, cooking items (empty food boxes), games, toys, travel brochures, ethnic restaurant menus, music tape, artwork, etc.

**Directions:**

1. Ask parents and children to donate some of the above objects or other items that reflect their culture. (Explain that the children will be playing with these things, so do not include anything valuable.)

2. Put the objects in a box with the child's name and the culture the items represent.

3. Let the children share their culture boxes with classmates.

4. Leave the box open for the children to investigate, or put the various objects in centers around the room. For example, cooking utensils and food boxes could go in the Dramatic Play area, books in the library, or a music tape in the Music Center.

**Variations:**

✏ Compare the items in different culture boxes. How are they alike? How are they different?

✏ Invite parents to read a book to the class in their native language. (They could also make a tape.)

# CLASS MUSEUM

Children will enjoy exploring the money, clothing, books, pictures, toys, and other objects in the class museum. "Hands-on" experiences will also spark interest and provide insight into other cultures.

*You will need:*
bookshelf or table
posterboard
markers
travel brochures
glue
scissors

*Directions:*

1. Make a sign from the posterboard that says "Class Museum." Decorate it with pictures from the travel brochures and hang it by the bookshelf or table.

2. Ask the children if they've ever been to a museum. What kinds of things can you find in a museum? Explain that your class can have its own museum where the children can share souvenirs, pictures, money, books, clothing, or other items they have from foreign countries.

3. As the children bring in different objects, have them explain the items to their classmates before placing them in the museum.

*Variations:*

✏ Ask parents to be classroom guest speakers and talk about their native culture or countries they have visited.

✏ Take the class on a field trip to a museum.

# THE FUN HOUSE

This book will present a variety of ways that families have fun together. Children will also explore how families are alike and different.

**You will need:**

two sheets of 12″ × 18″ posterboard
12″ × 18″ newsprint
crayons or markers
hole punch
book rings

**Directions:**

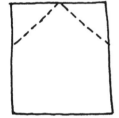

1. Cut the corners off the top of the posterboard and newsprint as shown to make the shape of a house.

2. Ask the children to tall how they have fun with their family. Emphasize that there are many different ways families have fun together.

3. Give each child a piece of newsprint and ask the children to draw a picture of how they have fun with their families.

4. Let the children dictate or write a sentence to go with their picture.

5. Put the pages together between the posterboard covers. Punch holes in the sides and insert the book rings. Decorate the cover and write "The Fun House."

6. Read the book to the class, pointing out how families are alike. Place the book in your library center.

**Variation:**

✏ Make books about how families work together, eat together, or help each other.

# CELEBRATE! CELEBRATE!

Children will gain respect for how different families celebrate. Everyone loves a party!

**You will need:**
language experience chart
markers
party decorations
food

**Directions:**

1. Ask the children to describe celebrations they have with their families.

2. Make a list on the chart of all the holidays and celebrations the children suggest. How are they alike? How are they different?

3. Let the children think of a unique classroom celebration they could have. It might be "Fabulous Friday," "Marvelous Me Day," a "Banana Split Bash," etc.

4. Divide the children into groups and let them plan the games, decorations, food, etc.

**Variations:**

✆ Each month let the children who have birthdays in that month plan a group party for the rest of the class. Those with July and August birthdays may plan a party with the June birthday children.

✆ Ask parents to visit your class and share a holiday celebration from their culture.

✆ Have every child bring in a picture (or video) of one of their family celebrations and tell classmates about it.

# PASS THE PARCEL

Here is a game children in England like to play at parties. Your class is sure to enjoy it, too!

**You will need:**

small box
tape
tissue paper or comics from the newspaper
one sticker or other goodie for each child
music

**Directions:**

1. Put the treats in the box and wrap a layer of tissue paper or funny papers around it.

2. Continue wrapping more layers around the box. (Ten layers work well. Or make enough layers so each child in the room can unwrap the package.)

3. Have the children sit in a circle and explain that this is a game children in England like to play at parties. It's called "Pass the Parcel" because in England people call a package a "parcel." The game is played by passing the package around the circle. When the music stops, whoever is holding the parcel may unwrap *one* layer. When the music starts, they must continue passing the parcel. (If it stops at a child who has already unwrapped a layer, then the package is passed to the next child who has not had a turn.)

4. Play the game until the last layer is unwrapped. The person holding the box may then pass out the goodies to the rest of the class.

5. Ask: "How do you think children in England are like you? "What game would you like to teach children in England?"

**Variations:**

✏ Let the children wrap the package for the game.

✏ Wrap a book, puzzle, or new toy the whole class can enjoy.

# PIÑATA PARTY

Piñatas are a party favorite of children in Central America and South America. Making a piñata and having a party will enable children to share a part of that culture.

**You will need:**
two paper plates
tissue paper
glue, markers, stapler, scissors
heavy string or rope
broomstick, blindfold
newspaper, tape
goodies (stickers, candy, balloons, etc.)

**Directions:**

1. Explain that many children in Central America and South America have piñatas at holiday celebrations and birthday parties. Tell the children that they can help you make a piñata for a classroom party.

2. Staple the paper plates together two-thirds of the way around. Let the children decorate the plates with tissue paper and markers. They can make an animal, person, flower, or holiday symbol.

3. Fill the paper plates with treats; then staple around the remainder of the way. Poke a hole in the top and tie on heavy string or rope. Attach the other end of the rope to the end of the broomstick.

4. Roll up several sheets of newspaper and tape to make a bat to hit at the piñata.

5. Blindfold one child at a time. Hand the child the bat; then turn the child around three times. Let the child try to hit the piñata as it is swung around. Every child gets a chance.

6. When the piñata is broken, divide the goodies among the children.

**Variations:**

✏ Let the children make individual piñatas. First, have them decorate a lunch bag with markers and tissue paper. Second, fill it with treats. Third, fold down the top of the sack over a piece of yarn and staple in place. Knot the ends of the yarn so it can be hung.

✏ Learn to play other games children in different parts of the world play.

# WHERE IN THE WORLD?

As children become aware of where some of their ancestors came from, they will also learn how to use the globe.

**You will need:**     globe

**Directions:**

1. Show the children the globe. Identify the land, water, the United States, where they live, and other meaningful locations.

2. Ask the children if they know what the word "ancestors" means. Explain that ancestors are their relatives who lived before them. Many of their ancestors came from other countries. If children know where their ancestors came from, point out those countries on the globe.

3. Give the children a "mission." Ask them to go home and find out from their parents where their ancestors came from.

4. Continue identifying countries on the globe as children find out about their ancestors.

5. Conclude by emphasizing that most of us have a combination of ethnic backgrounds. "How are all people alike?" "How are we different?" "Why do we say that it's 'a small world'?"

**Variations:**

✏ Put up a map of the United States (or world). Ask the children to find out where they were born; then mark it on the map with their name and a pushpin.

✏ Plan a "Heritage Day" where children dress up in the native dress of the country their ancestors came from.

# PEN PALS

What an exciting way to foster writing skills and make a new friend in another area of the country.

**You will need:**

paper
pencils
pens
stamps
envelopes

**Directions:**

1.  Contact the Pen Pal Program sponsored by the Association for Childhood Education International at the address below:

    ACEI Pen Pal Program
    11501 Georgia Avenue, Suite 315
    Wheaton, MD 20902
    Phone: 800-423-3563

2.  Give each child in your classroom a pen pal from the class you are paired with. Set aside a time for the children to write letters to each other.

**Variations:**

✎ Pen Pals are also available through the Internet on the Student Letter Exchange:

http://www.pen-pal.com/index.html

✎ Visual Pen Pals, an international children's art exchange, can be reached at:

http://www.mediacity.com/~anaylor/schoolpal.html

# PEOPLE COLLAGE

As children cut out pictures of people from magazines, they will become aware of the wide variety of physical attributes that people have. When they put them together to create a collage, they will discover how very much we are alike.

***You will need:***

mirror
old magazines, catalogs, newspapers
scissors
glue
3′ × 9′ sheet of butcher paper

***Directions:***

1. Begin a discussion by passing around a mirror and asking the children if they all look the same. How are they different? (Include hair, eyes, skin, size, and so forth.)

2. Pass out a magazine to each child or to small groups of children. Ask them to find as many different kinds of people as they can and cut them out. Challenge them to find people of different ages, sexes, and with different physical characteristics.

3. Have the children glue their people to the butcher paper to create a giant "people collage."

4. Hang the collage in the classroom and ask the children to point out differences in the people. How are the people in the collage the same? What would the world be like if everyone looked the same?

***Variations:***

✏ Cut a large circle out of posterboard and make a collage of different faces.

✏ Give children crayons, paints, and markers to create their own "people collage."

✏ Let children make books in which they can glue pictures of many different people.

# PAPER DOLL PARADE

Children will learn about the concept of "different" as they take paper dolls that are alike and make them unique and different.

*You will need:*    24″ × 7″ newsprint or other thin paper

crayons and markers (body colors)

scissors

*Directions:*

1. Demonstrate how to make paper dolls by folding the paper in half, then fourths, then eighths.

2. Using the guide at the bottom of the page, cut out the body shape, being careful not to cut the paper apart at the hands. (An adult will need to cut these out for younger children.)

3. Hold up the paper dolls. "Do all people look like this? Look around the room and see how different we all are!"

4. Give each child some paper dolls, markers, and crayons. Challenge them to make all their dolls look different.

5. Let the children show their paper dolls when they are finished. Hang them around the room so they are all holding hands in a "paper doll parade."

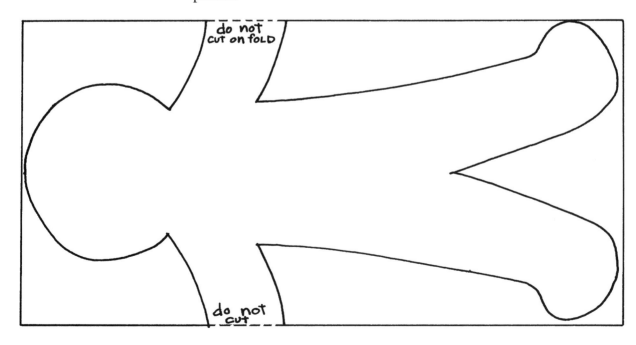

# PEOPLE PLAY DOUGH

Children always enjoy squishing, squeezing, and molding with play dough. This recipe is particularly good because children can make many different people.

**You will need:**
2 cups all-purpose flour
1 cup salt
2 cups water
2 tablespoons cream of tartar
2 tablespoons vegetable oil or baby oil
saucepan
measuring spoons and cups
cinnamon, curry powder, cocoa, ginger, chili powder, paprika

**Directions:**

1. Stir the first five ingredients together until smooth.

2. Cook over medium heat until a soft ball forms and sticks to the spoon.

3. Remove from heat and knead until smooth.

4. Divide the dough into four equal balls. Poke a hole in the center of each ball; then sprinkle in one of the above spices. (Experiment to get the shade you like.)

5. Squeeze until the color is blended in the dough.

6. Let the children mold people with the different doughs.

7. Store the dough in airtight containers.

**Variations:**

✎ Dissolve instant coffee in the water before adding it to the other dry ingredients.

✎ Experiment with other spices, paints, and food colorings.

✎ Give the children wiggly eyes to put in their play dough people.

✎ For a hard-drying dough, mix 4 cups flour, 1 cup salt, and 1-1/2 cups water. Bake in a slow oven or air dry. Paint with body color tempera.

**Hint:**
The first five steps under "Directions" must be done by an adult. Be sure the children stay away from the heat source.

# THAT'S MY BABY

More than the sensory pleasure the children will derive from the water and bubbles, they will begin to explore how people are alike and different.

***You will need:***    plastic tubs or water table

wash cloths, towels, bar soap, baby powder, etc.

washable dolls

***Directions:***

1.  Send a note home to parents asking them to send a washable baby doll with their child on a particular day. (If possible, have a few extra dolls on hand for those who forget, or let children share their baby with a friend.)

2.  Have children bring their babies to group time. Encourage them to tell their baby's name or other special information. Ask them to describe their baby's eyes. Next talk about the different kinds of hair their babies have. Look at their baby's skin. Is it like theirs? How else are their babies different? How are they alike?

3.  Let the children bathe their babies and play in the water in small groups. Provide towels, baby powder, and other props for caring for babies.

***Variations:***

✆  This is a fun outdoor activity on a warm day.

✆  Let children have a "tea party" with their babies or prepare a special snack for them.

✆  Provide children with dolls reflective of different ethnic groups in the Housekeeping area.

✆  Encourage children to talk about what they were like when they were babies and how they've changed.

# "DIVERSITY DAY" BODY PUPPETS

Diversity Day will focus on some nontraditional heroes and heroines who have contributed to our country. These people can also serve as good models for the children.

***You will need:***

one paper grocery bag for each child
crayons and markers
scissors
glue
hole punch
scrap paper, collage materials
yarn

***Directions:***

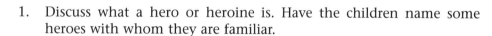

1. Discuss what a hero or heroine is. Have the children name some heroes with whom they are familiar.

2. Ask the children to think of a famous person who they would like to learn more about. Encourage them to select a male or female from their ethnic background, or perhaps someone who has overcome a disability.

3. Take the children to the school library to do research, or ask their parents to help them learn more about their hero or heroine.

4. Give each child a grocery bag to make a body puppet of their hero. Use the bottom of the bag as the head; then decorate it with markers, yarn, and other collage materials.

5. Poke two holes in the top corners. Tie on an 18-inch piece of yarn.

6. On Diversity Day, let the children wear their body puppets as they tell their classmates about their famous person and why they admire him or her.

***Variation:***

✏ Older children might enjoy writing stories to go along with their puppets.

# COMPARE ME

By doing comparisons, children will develop math skills and increase their self-awareness.

**You will need:**   chart paper
markers

**Directions:**   1.   Write the following questions on the chart paper:

> **Compare Me**
>
> What is larger than you?
> What is smaller than you?
>
> What is older than you?
> What is younger than you?
>
> What is heavier than you?
> What is lighter than you?
>
> What is stronger than you?
> What is weaker than you?
>
> What is faster than you?
> What is slower than you?

2.   Read the list one question at a time, giving the children an opportunity to suggest possible answers. (Accept divergent answers.)

3.   Conclude by asking children how they are like other people. How are they different from other people? "What's good about being just the way you are?"

**Variations:**   ✏   Have older children copy the questions and write their comparisons.

✏   Let younger children draw pictures to illustrate the different comparisons.

# PEOPLE GRAPH

Similarities and differences will be explored as match concepts are reinforced.

**You will need:**

large chart paper
crayons (regular and multicultural)
yardstick
marker
mirror

**Directions:**

1. Divide the paper into a grid as shown below.

2. Label the top sections with "Eyes," "Hair," "Skin," "Lips," and "Teeth." Write the children's names along the side.

3. Discuss some of the ways people are alike and ways they are different. Show the children the graph and explain that they can fill in the squares with different colors to represent how different parts of them look.

4. Give the children crayons and let them color in the squares by their name with the appropriate color. (Provide them with a mirror so they can look at themselves.)

5. Use the graph to make comparisons.

**Variation:**

✆ Do a similar graph of how many brothers, sisters, pets, grandparents, etc., each child has.

| People Graph | | | | | |
|---|---|---|---|---|---|
| | Eyes | Hair | Skin | Lips | Teeth |
| Siui | | | | | |
| David | | | | | |
| Ariel | | | | | |
| Jung | | | | | |
| Paula | | | | | |
| Ron | | | | | |
| Katrina | | | | | |
| Jim | | | | | |

# GROUPIES

As children think about all the different groups they belong to, they will gain insight into the commonalties so many of us share.

**You will need:**
large paper
pencils, pens, or crayons

**Directions:**

1. Lead the children in a discussion of what a group is. Ask them to suggest some different groups to which they belong (i.e., male, female, family, ethnic, neighborhood, club, church, sport, etc.). Can you belong to more than one group at the same time?

2. Give each child a large sheet of paper. Have the children write their names in the middle. Next, ask them to write or draw pictures of all the groups to which they belong.

3. Let the children share their pictures with classmates. Then hang them in the room.

**Variations:**

✏ Make a composite list of all the different groups the children come up with.

✏ Ask the children which group is their favorite. Why? Which group are they most proud of belonging to?

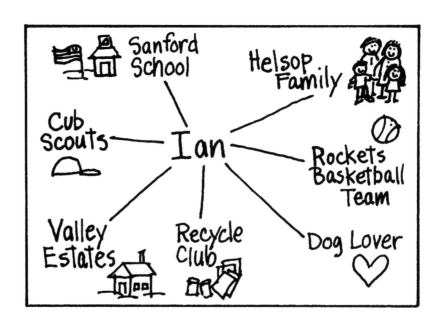

# OLYMPIC DAY

Children will develop physical skills as they learn about different countries around the world.

**You will need:**

globe
toilet paper roll
aluminum foil
yellow cellophane or tissue paper
cardboard cut into 4" circles
hole punch, scissors, glue
ribbon or yarn
riding toys
balls, hula hoops, jump ropes, beanbags
climbing equipment

**Directions:**

1. Make an "Olympic torch" by wrapping aluminum foil around the toilet paper roll. Scallop the tissue paper or cellophane to look like fire and glue it in the toilet paper roll.

2. Gather the children around the globe. Show them the torch and ask them what they know about the Olympic Games. Explain that your class can have their own Olympic Games on the playground.

3. Let each child look at the globe and choose a country he or she would like to represent.

4. Set up different stations on the playground similar to those below. (Write the numerals 1 through 7 on paper and tape them near these different "events.")

   1 — Bounce the ball 20 times.
   2 — Toss the beanbags at a target.
   3 — Ride a tricycle.
   4 — Climb up and slide down the climber.
   5 — Hula hoop.
   6 — Jump rope.
   7 — Running, jumping, galloping, and skipping relays.

5. Take the children on the playground and demonstrate how to do the above "events." (Emphasize the fun of participating and eliminate competition.)

6. When you return to the classroom, let each child make a medal by covering a cardboard circle with aluminum foil. Punch a hole and string with a 24-inch piece of ribbon.

**Variations:**

✏ Have an awards ceremony in which each child stands on a crate or large wooden block as his or her medal is hung around his or her neck.

✏ Let the children do research on the country they are representing. They might make flags, make a poster, or do other projects.

# SHARE AND CARE

Developing empathy and learning to share with others less fortunate will be nurtured with these projects.

**You will need:**    materials appropriate for each project

**Directions:**

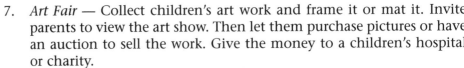

1.  *Clothes Drive* — Have the children bring in clothes they have outgrown to pass on to a shelter or needy family.

2.  *Pantry Party* — Ask the children to bring in canned foods and nonperishables to contribute to a food bank.

3.  *Trim the Tree* — Let children bring in hats and mittens to decorate the classroom Christmas tree or Hanukkah bush. Then distribute the items to the homeless.

4.  *Toy Time* — Ask the children to bring in their old toys. Let them play with the old toys and clean them up before distributing to a children's shelter.

5.  *Senior Center* — Take the children to a retirement center to sing songs or put on skits. Have the children make a special snack or art project to share with the seniors.

6.  *Adopt a Grandparent* — Contact a nursing home and "adopt" an older person who can visit your class once a week to read, talk, or play with your students.

7.  *Art Fair* — Collect children's art work and frame it or mat it. Invite parents to view the art show. Then let them purchase pictures or have an auction to sell the work. Give the money to a children's hospital or charity.

8.  *Disaster Crew* — If there is a disaster locally or in another part of the country, suggest the children collect food, money, or clothes to help.

# SPECIAL TOOLS

Experimenting with crutches, hearing aids, prostheses, and other adaptive equipment will help children feel more comfortable around people who use these tools.

**You will need:**    pictures of people with physical challenges
crutches
wheelchair
hearing aid
prostheses
corrective glasses
braces

**Directions:**
1. Contact local agencies or ask parents to share the above adaptive equipment with your classroom.

2. Introduce each piece of equipment to the class. Encourage the children to tell how it is used and how it helps people. Ask them to talk about friends they have who use these tools.

3. Include the equipment in the Dramatic Play center for the children to role-play with.

**Variations:**

- Hang pictures in the classroom of people with physical challenges.

- Include books in your classroom library about people with special needs.

- Invite siblings, relatives, or friends of the children to visit your classroom to talk about their special needs.

# READING HANDS

Recognizing Braille and understanding how people who are visually impaired "see with their hands" will be the goal of this project.

**You will need:**  copy of Braille alphabet on the following page
posterboard
markers
cup lids, books, and other examples of Braille
glue, heavy paper
dried lentils or split peas

**Directions:**

1. Enlarge the Braille alphabet on the posterboard.

2. Pass around the examples of Braille. Ask the children if they know what it is. Where else have they seen Braille used? How do people who are usually impaired "read" with their hands?

3. Give each child a handful of dried lentils or split peas and challenge them to reproduce some of the Braille letters. Ask them to spell out their name in Braille and glue it to the paper.

**Variations:**

✐ Have the children do crayon rubbings of the Braille cup lids or Braille in your school building.

✐ Invite someone who is visually impaired to talk to your class.

✐ How are canes and Seeing Eye dogs used to help people who are blind?

# Braille Alphabet

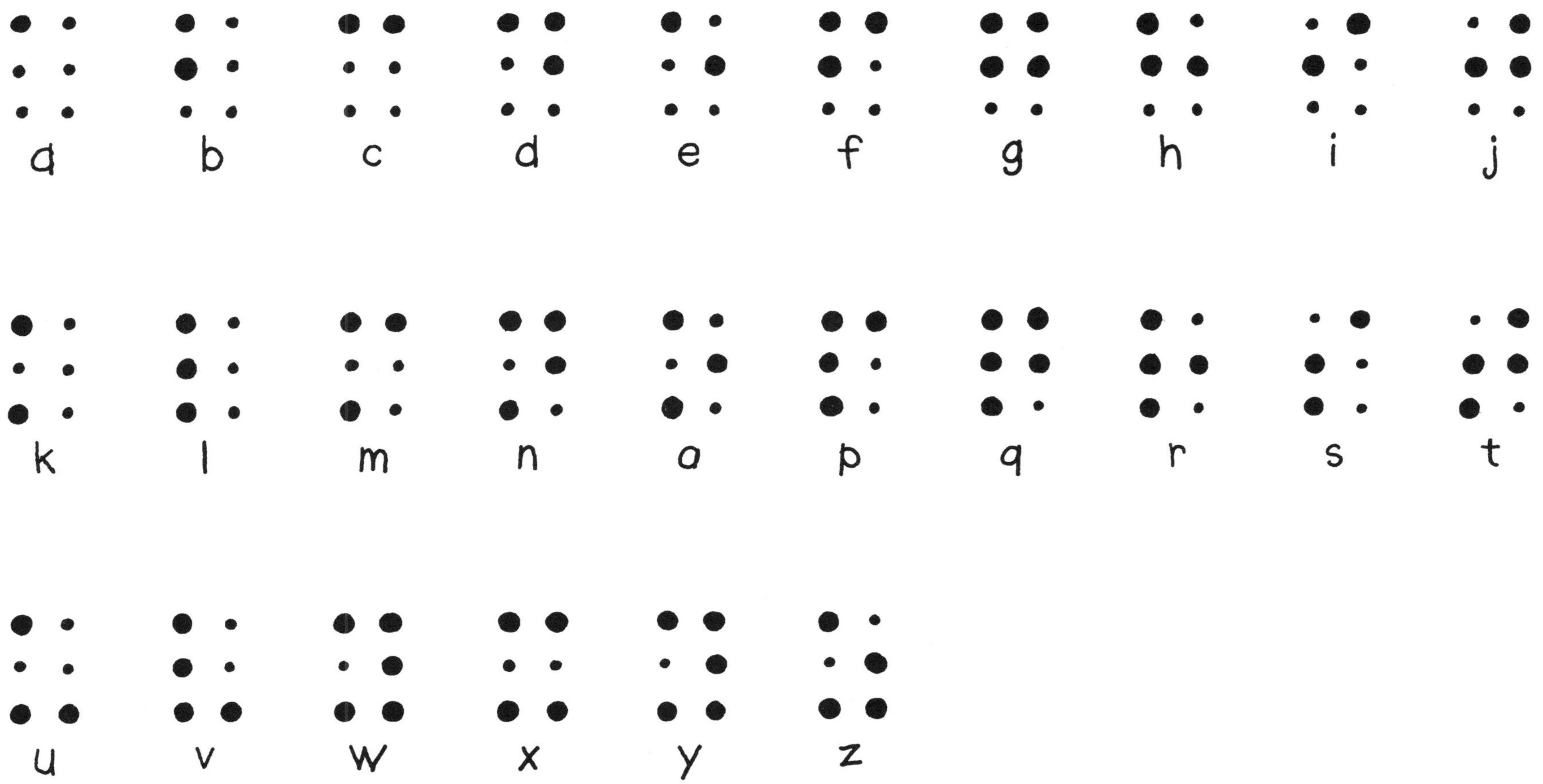

# SPEAKING HANDS

Children's sensitivity to people with hearing disabilities and their understanding of different ways people communicate will increase with this activity.

***You will need:***

copy of the American Manual Alphabet on the following page

posterboard, markers

glue, scissors

3" × 5" cards

***Directions:***

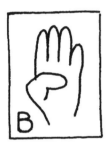

1. Use a copy machine to enlarge the letters on the following page. Make two copies. Glue one letter on the posterboard, and glue the other letter on an index card.

2. Ask the children if they know anyone who can't hear or speak. How do those people talk to each other? Explain that "sign language" is used so that people can communicate with their hands.

3. Display the posterboard and practice reproducing the letters with the children.

4. Pass out the individual letters signs to the children. As you call out the letters, the child holding that card may come up and match his or her card with the same sign on the poster.

***Variations:***

✎ Learn to sing the alphabet song or another song in sign language.

✎ Teach children simple signs for classroom directions, such as lining up, washing hands, sitting down, "no," etc.

✎ Help children learn how to sign their names.

✎ Invite someone with a hearing disability to talk to your class. (A child within your school would be a special guest.)

✎ Let the children examine a hearing aid. Explain how it makes the sound louder, although it is often not clear.

# AMERICAN MANUAL ALPHABET

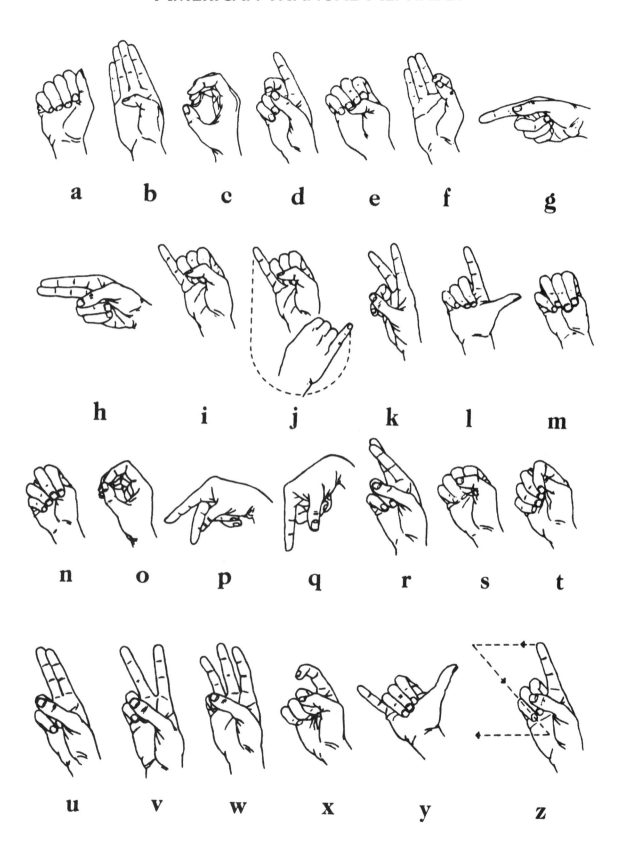

a b c d e f g

h i j k l m

n o p q r s t

u v w x y z

# WHAT'S IT LIKE?

By experiencing the frustrations of a disability, children will develop empathy for people with special needs.

**You will need:**
paper grocery bag
wax paper
scissors
masking tape

**Directions:**

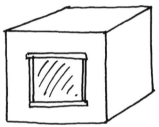

1. Make a vision mask so children can experience what it is like to be visually impaired. Cut 8 inches off the top of a grocery bag. Cut a 7-inch square out of one side of the bag and tape wax paper over the opening.

2. Let children take turns wearing the mask as they try to read, draw a picture, eat, etc.

3. Have the children cover their ears with their hands to see what it is like to have an auditory problem.

4. Tape the children's thumbs to their hands; then ask them to work a puzzle or put on their shoes. This will help them understand how difficult life can be with a physical handicap.

5. Conclude by having children share what it was like to have trouble seeing, hearing, or using their hands. How can they help people who have special needs?

**Variation:**
✏ Read stories to the children of people who have overcome physical limitations.

# A CIRCLE OF FRIENDS

The importance of everyone joining hands and working together will be highlighted with this activity.

**You will need:**

paper

markers

tape

**Directions:**

1. Write each of the following characters on a separate sheet of paper:

   | | | | |
   |---|---|---|---|
   | mother | doctor | astronaut | police officer |
   | grandfather | teacher | teenager | baby |
   | artist | builder | cook | music star |

2. Ask for volunteers to be each of the characters and tape their title on them.

3. Challenge the characters to line up in the order of their importance. Invite the audience to give input.

4. After watching the children argue about their importance for several minutes, tell all of them to join hands and form a circle.

5. Why does a circle solve their problem? Is any person more important than another person? Why should all people join hands in a circle of friendship?

**Variations:**

✎ Adapt the number of characters and their professions to those with whom your children are familiar.

✎ Give children other problem-solving situations that focus on the value of all human beings and how we need each other.

# 5

# Changes

Living in our rapidly changing society is difficult for adults, as it is for the young as well. Children today are faced with challenges, decisions, insecurities, and violence never dreamed of a generation ago. As educators, we can help prepare children by teaching them how to protect themselves, how to care for their bodies, and what to do in emergency situations. We must also focus on the future by showing children how to set and accomplish goals. Adaptability and inner strength are other skills that will give children hope and direction for tomorrow.

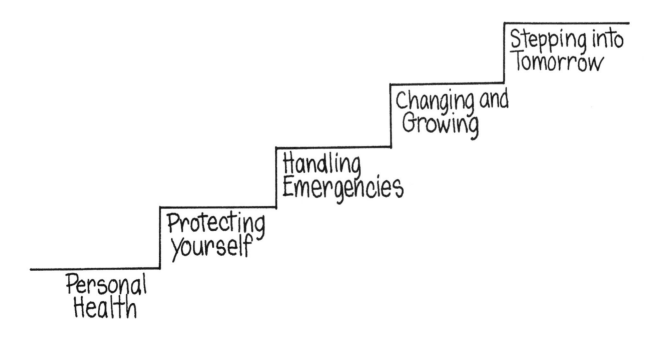

Stepping into Tomorrow

Changing and Growing

Handling Emergencies

Protecting Yourself

Personal Health

# FITNESS TRAIL

There is a positive relationship between self-esteem and how children look and feel. By discussing the importance of fitness and making an exercise trail, children will start developing lifelong health skills. They will also use social skills, language skills, and math skills as they create a fitness trail.

***You will need:***

several sheets of 12″ × 18″ posterboard or cardboard

markers

tape

***Directions:***

1. Involve the children in a discussion about the importance of exercise. "How does exercise help your body?" "What happens to you if you don't exercise?"

2. Brainstorm all the different ways that people exercise.

3. Ask children if they have ever seen a fitness trail. Describe how a fitness trail is like a walk with different exercises that you can perform as you go along.

4. Have the children demonstrate various exercises a person might do along a fitness trail.

5. Divide the children into small groups and give them a piece of posterboard. Let each group make a sign for the trail by illustrating an exercise and suggesting the number of times it can be done.

6. Take the children outside and let them hang the signs around the playground to create their own fitness trail. Encourage the children to follow the trail and do the exercises.

***Variations:***

✆ Laminate the cards to make them more permanent. Or use wood scraps and paints to make signs.

✆ On rainy days, create an exercise trail in your school gym or hallway.

✆ Invite a personal trainer or other fitness professional to talk about the benefits of exercise to the children.

✆ Take a field trip to a health spa or fitness center.

# HEALTHY FOODS

Children will begin to explore nutritious foods and healthy diets as they create this collage.

**You will need:**
real or play food (use a combination of healthy foods like fruits, vegetables, and cereals, and junk foods such as sodas, candies, and chips)

two paper grocery bags

old magazines or grocery store advertisements

paper plates

crayons, markers

scissors, glue

**Directions:**

1. Place the foods in front of the children. Explain that some foods are good for our bodies and give us energy to play, think, and grow strong. Other foods are full of sugar or fat and are not good for us to eat.

2. Tell the children that they are going to play a game to learn which foods they should choose to eat. On one grocery bag print "Healthy Foods" and on the other bag print "Junk Foods."

3. Hold up the foods one at a time as the children tell you which bag they should go in.

4. Give each child a paper plate. Ask the children to cut out magazine pictures of foods that are good for them to eat and give them on the plate. They can also draw pictures of healthy foods.

**Variations:**

✏ Have a "Healthy Tasting Party" where children bring fruits, vegetables, breads, cheeses, and other nutritious foods to share with their friends.

✏ Make a language experience chart of healthy snack foods they should eat.

✏ Ask the children to keep a food diary by writing all the foods they eat for a week. Have them evaluate their diets.

# TOOTH TALK

The importance of brushing teeth and eating healthy foods will be emphasized with "tooth talk."

**You will need:**

white posterboard
scissors, markers
toothbrush, toothpaste

**Directions:**

1. Use the pattern below to cut out a tooth puppet from white posterboard.

2. Put your fingers through the holes and dance "Happy Tooth" in front of you as you sing this song to "Row Your Boat."

> Brush, brush, brush your teeth.
> Brush them every day.
> Brush them up and brush them down.
> Keep decay away.

3. Ask the children why it is important for them to brush their teeth. Discuss what happens if you don't brush your teeth.

4. Demonstrate proper brushing techniques by brushing down on the top teeth and up on the bottom teeth.

**Variations:**

- Let the children make their own tooth puppets.

- Invite a dentist to talk to your class about dental health.

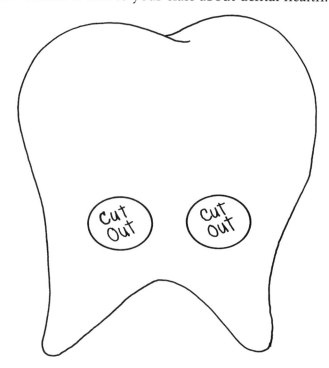

# GOOD NIGHT!

The importance of rest and relaxation for good health will be emphasized with this activity.

**You will need:**
one sheet of 9″ × 12″ construction paper
9″ × 6″ fabric scraps
crayons
scissors
glue
paper cut in 3-inch circles

**Directions:**

1. Ask the children what would happen if they had a toy with a battery that they left on and never turned off. Relate how their bodies need to be "turned off" sometimes, too, such as when they rest or go to sleep. Discuss what happens when they don't get enough sleep.

2. Have the children share what time they go to bed and their bedtime routines.

3. Give each child a sheet of paper and let them choose a piece of fabric to glue on the bottom half of the paper to be their blanket.

4. Ask them to draw their bed on the top half.

5. Give each child a circle and have them draw what their face looks like when they are asleep. Glue the face above the covers.

6. Let the children show their pictures and tell classmates what they do when they can't fall asleep.

**Variation:**
✏ Let the children act out putting a doll to bed.

# SCRUB-A-DUB

Washing hands is a simple way to prevent illnesses in your classroom, and it will be more fun with this song.

**You will need:**    no materials are needed

**Directions:**

1. Discuss the importance of washing hands with the children. Ask them what happens if they don't wash their hands.

2. Make a list of all the times when they should wash their hands, such as before eating, after toileting, after blowing their nose, etc.

3. Demonstrate the correct way to wash hands following the steps below:

   a. Wet hands.
   b. Squirt (or rub) on soap.
   c. Scrub hands.
   d. Rinse hands.
   e. Dry hands.
   f. Turn off water with paper towel.
   g. Throw towel in trash.

4. Teach children this song to the tune of "Ring Around the Rosie":

   > Scrub-a-dub your hands.
   > Scrub-a-dub your hands.
   > Germs, germs,
   > Go down the drain.

**Variations:**

- Discuss the importance of bathing at home.

- Put a sign on the back of the bathroom door similar to the one below:

- Cut a raw potato in half. Ask one child to rub his or her hands over one half. Ask another child to wash his or her hands before rubbing them on the other potato half. Label the potatoes "clean hands" and "dirty hands" and observe for several days. What happens?

# MANNERS AND MAGIC WORDS

Adults and friends respond more favorably to children who have manners and use common courtesies.

**You will need:**

chart paper
markers

**Directions:**

☆Magic Words☆

Please.
Thank you.
Excuse Me.
May I?
Pardon me.
I'm sorry.

1. Have one child come to the front of the room. Pretend to run into that child and push him or her. Ask the children how they would feel if someone did that to them. What should you say if you accidentally bump into someone? Choose another child to role-play the scene saying, "Excuse me."

2. Give a child a toy; then grab it back from him or her. Ask the children how they would feel, and to suggest a better way to ask for something you want. Choose another child to act out the scene and say, "Please."

3. Have a child get a book for you. Take it from him or her without saying anything. Let the children suggest what you should say when someone does something nice for you. Ask a child to role-play a similar situation saying, "Thank you."

4. Write "Magic Words" on the chart paper and ask the children to think of words they should use to be polite. Write the words on the chart.

5. Read the list and have the children give you examples of how they would use the words. Conclude by discussing how you feel when other people are polite to you and respect you.

**Variations:**

✏ Use a play telephone to teach children telephone courtesies.

✏ During snacks, lunch, and other "teachable times," help children with table manners.

# EMERGENCY! EMERGENCY! 911

Knowing what to do in emergency situations will help children feel independent and confident. It may also save their lives!

***You will need:***      play telephone
crayons or markers
self-stick labels

***Directions:***

1. Describe several emergency situations and ask the children what they would do. For example, what would they do if they saw someone get hit by a car? If they saw a fire? etc.

2. Show the children the play telephone and demonstrate how to call for help using the 911 emergency service. (If your community does not have 911, then teach children other appropriate numbers to call for help.)

3. Let the children take turns pretending how they would act in emergency situations by dialing 911 on the play phone.

4. Give the children the address labels on which to write 911 or other emergency numbers. Tell them to place them on their phones at home in case they ever have an accident or problem.

***Variations:***

    ✆ Invite a police officer, firefighter, or other safety official to speak to your class about safety precautions and emergency procedures.

    ✆ After you practice fire drills, tornado drills, or earthquake drills at school, have the children brainstorm what they would do at home in a similar situation.

# WHAT IF?

By problem solving how to handle emergencies or scary situations, children will feel more confident and empowered.

**You will need:**   no materials are needed

**Directions:**

1. Ask the children to play the "What If" game with you. They are to think of how they would handle the situations below. Encourage the children to offer alternative ways of handling each problem.

   — What if a stranger tries to make you get in his or her car? What if the stranger offers you candy or tells you your mother said you should go with him or her?

   — What if someone offers you some drugs? What if someone tries to get you to smoke a cigarette with him or her?

   — What if you are in the store and your friend tells you to put a candy bar in your pocket and to not pay for it?

   — What if you wake up in the middle of the night and smell smoke in your house?

   — What if you go to the mall and get lost?

   — What if you and a friend are riding bikes and your friend falls off his or her bike and gets hurt?

2. Have the children role-play the above situations.

3. Let the children share personal problems or fears they have. Ask their friends to suggest how they would handle these situations.

**Variations:**

   ✏ Act out what to do if they hear gun shots by dropping to the ground and lying flat.

   ✏ Cut out magazine or newspaper articles involving children. Have the children problem-solve what to do in similar circumstances.

# CHOICES

Making good choices and dealing with the consequences is a challenge throughout life. By role-playing different situations children might face, they will be better prepared to make the "right choice."

***You will need:***      puppet or stuffed animal

***Directions:***

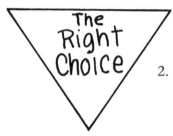

1. Gather the children in a small or large group. Ask them if they've ever had to make a choice. Discuss how we sometimes make good choices, but other times we make poor choices. Have the children give examples of good choices they've made; then let them share bad choices they've made.

2. Introduce the puppet to the children and tell them his name is Charlie Choice. Explain that Charlie is confused because he doesn't know how to make good choices, but perhaps the children can help him.

3. Think of different situations similar to the ones below. Then ask the children to tell Charlie what he should do. Encourage them to tell why and describe the consequences of different choices.

    a. You are playing with a little toy at school that you really like a lot. Should you put the toy in your pocket and take it home? Why or why not?

    b. Your big brother makes you very angry. He's been working hard on a model airplane. Should you mess up his model? Why or why not?

    c. You accidentally break the computer in your classroom. Should you tell the teacher? Why or why not?

    d. Your mother tells you not to watch a certain television show, but she leaves the house. Should you watch it anyway? Why or why not?

4. Summarize by encouraging the children to think about the consequences of their choices before doing something. Explain that they can always talk to their parents, teacher, or another adult if they are confused about what they should do.

***Variations:***

  ✏ Let the children role-play the above situations.

  ✏ Review choices different characters make in stories you read to the class. Evaluate their choices.

# YES OR NO

Here's a game to play to give children more practice in making choices.

**You will need:**
construction paper
markers or crayons
scissors
tape
craft sticks

**Directions:**

1. Using the patterns at the bottom of the page, cut out two circles for each child.

2. Let the children color the faces ( ☺ or ☹ ) with markers or crayons.

3. Tape the faces to the craft sticks.

4. Discuss the importance of making good choices. Sometimes you should say "Yes" (hold up the ☺ ), and sometimes you should say "No" (hold up the ☹ ). Tell stories similar to these:

   Your best friend says, "Let's throw rocks at cars."

   You are playing in the Blocks Center and a friend asks if he or she can play with you.

   You copy from a classmate's paper during test.

5. Ask the children "why" they made certain decisions.

**Variation:**

✏ Let the children make up their own stories for their classmates to respond to.

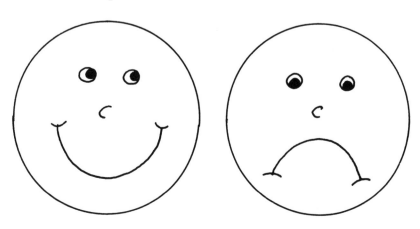

# I SAY "NO!"

If and when children are confronted with drugs, they will know the correct response they should make.

**You will need:**
paper
crayons or markers

**Directions:**

1. Discuss what drugs are. Explain the difference between medicine that you take when you are sick and illegal drugs. Emphasize that they should only take medicine from their parents or a nurse or doctor.

2. Ask the children what happens to people who take illegal drugs.

3. Have one child pretend to be a drug dealer and try to talk another child into taking drugs. Teach the children to yell, "No! Go away!"

4. Have the children suggest who they should tell if someone offers them drugs.

**Variations:**

✏ For additional information on the D.A.R.E. program, call your local police department. The "Just Say No" Foundation is another source for information (800-258-2766).

✏ Show the children the universal sign for poison and caution them about playing with bottles or cans with that symbol.

**Hint:**
Be sensitive to children's family situations. Some of them may have home experiences with family members on drugs.

# DON'T TOUCH!

Personal protection and learning to say "no" are critical skills that children will practice with this activity.

**You will need:**     doll with clothes
crayons and paper

**Directions:**
1. Begin the discussion by making up a story about the doll similar to the one below:

    "This is Amy and she's six years old. One day this person in her neighborhood came up to her and tried to touch her in a place she didn't like. What should Amy do?"

2. Ask the children to finish the story and give their suggestions for handling the problem. Have them name parts of their body where it's okay if other people touch them. Remind them that where their bathing suit covers them is "don't touch!"

3. Act out saying "NO" and telling another adult if someone makes them feel uncomfortable or tries to touch them in a personal area.

4. Give the children paper and crayons and have them draw their body with their bathing suit on. Ask them to show you on their pictures where it's okay to be touched.

**Variations:**
✏ Invite a school counselor or psychologist to talk to your class about personal safety.

✏ Contact the National Child Abuse Hotline at 800-422-4453 for additional information.

# PICTURE SEQUENCE

The life cycle of human beings will be presented as children sequence photos.

**You will need:**

photos of people at different states in life (for example, infant, toddler, preschooler, school age, teenager, young adult, adult, older adult—try to include males and females from different ethnic groups)

construction paper

scissors

glue

**Directions:**

1. Use family photos or cut out pictures of the life stages from catalogs and magazines.

2. Glue the photos or pictures to construction paper.

3. Display the photos or pictures in front of the children. Which one looks the youngest? Which one looks like the next to the youngest? Continue having the children sequence the pictures from left to right.

4. Mix up the photos or pictures and let the children sequence them independently.

5. Discuss how babies act, toddlers act, and other things people do at different stages.

**Variations:**

- Collect several different dolls (baby, preschooler, adult) for the children to sequence.

- Have the children sequence shoes of different sizes, such as a bootie, toddler shoe, sneaker, high heel.

- Give children pictures of the life cycle of animals to sequence, such as a caterpillar to butterfly or tadpole to frog.

# WHEN I WAS A BABY

As they construct this book, children will focus on how they have grown and changed. They will also be using reading and writing skills.

**You will need:**
one 6″ × 36″ strip of butcher paper for each child
markers or crayons

**Directions:**

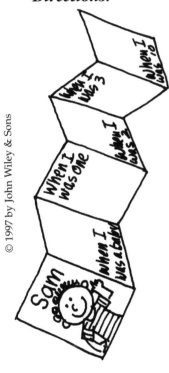

1. Ask the children to describe what they were like when they were a baby. What silly things did they do? How have they changed?

2. Give each child a strip of paper and demonstrate how to fold it in half. Then fold it in thirds to create six sections.

3. Open the paper and fold it back and forth in accordion fashion to create a fold-out book.

4. Have the children draw their face in the first section.

5. On the second section, they should write "When I was a baby . . ." and draw a picture of themselves as a baby.

6. On the third section, they write "When I was one . . ." and draw themselves as a toddler.

7. Continue writing different ages and drawing appropriate pictures.

8. On the last page, have the children draw what they think they will be like when they are grown up.

**Variations:**

✏ Let older children write a sentence about themselves on each page at various ages.

✏ Use the fold-out book for other sequencing activities and creative stories.

# BABY, LOOK AT ME NOW!

With this project children will measure, compare, and delight at "how big" they have become.

**You will need:**
baby photos
baby blankets
large plastic ziplock bags
sand, shovels
scale, tape measure

**Directions:**

1. Several days before doing this project, ask parents to send in a baby photo of their child along with their child's weight and height at birth on the back of the photo. Also ask them to send in a baby blanket their child used if they still have one.

2. Let the children take turns sharing their photos and talking about how they've changed since they were born.

3. Let the children find how tall they were when they were born on the tape measure. Compare it with their height now.

4. Put books or blocks on the scale to show how much they weighed when they were born. Then weigh them now and compare.

5. Take the children outside and let them fill a ziplock bag with sand until it weighs approximately what they did at birth. Have them wrap it up in their baby blanket and carry it around so they can see how they felt as a baby.

**Variations:**

- Have the children carry around their "sand babies" for a day so they can see how much responsibility a baby is.

- Children will also enjoy seeing a photo of their teacher as a baby!

- Ask children to bring in books, toys, or other objects they played with when there were a baby. How have their interests changed?

- Record children's height and weight on a growth chart so they can see how much they are growing and changing.

# NOW I CAN POP-UP

By identifying something they have learned to do, children will feel proud and confident.

**You will need:**

12″ × 9″ construction paper
scissors
crayons
glue
scrap paper

**Directions:**

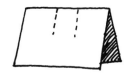

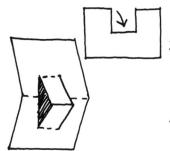

1.  Ask the children to think about something they couldn't do when they were younger, but they can do now. Have them complete this sentence, "I couldn't _____, but now I can _____." (For example, "I couldn't tie my shoes, but now I can," or "I couldn't ride a bike, but now I can.")

2.  Demonstrate how to take the construction paper and fold it in half. On the fold, cut two 2-inch slits in the middle as shown. Bend the tab in to make a pop-up.

3.  Have the children draw and cut out a picture of themselves from the scrap paper. (This picture should be 3 or 4 inches tall, or about the size of their first.) Glue this to the tab so it will "pop-up" when the card is opened.

4.  On the front of the card ask the children to complete this sentence, "I couldn't _____." On the inside write, "But now I can _____."

**Variations:**

✏ This is a good project for the children to do at the end of the school year to help them focus on all their accomplishments.

✏ Let the children make a pop-up of what they want to be when they grow up.

# DOES THE SHOE FIT?

**This shoe will be a keepsake for the children and will be a reminder of how much they are growing.**

***You will need:***
variety of shoes worn by different ages (baby, toddler, preschooler, school-age, teenager, and adult)

one old shoe from each child

gallon of white school glue

wax paper

old paintbrush

gold or silver spray paint

newspaper

***Directions:***

1. Several days before doing this activity, send home a note to the parents asking them to send in one old shoe their child has outgrown. (Sneakers work best.)

2. Have the children bring their old shoes to a group meeting. Place the collection of baby through adult shoes on the floor. Hold up the shoes one at a time, asking the children who might wear the shoe. Could they wear the shoe? Why or why not?

3. Tell the children that they're going to "preserve" their shoe so it will last a long time, and they can look at it and remind themselves how much they are growing.

4. Cover a table with newspapers. Let the children paint a layer of school glue inside, outside, and all over the shoe. Dry for several days on wax paper.

5. Paint a second coat of glue on the shoe and dry.

6. Spray paint the shoe gold or silver. (The teacher should do this.) Date the shoe on the bottom.

***Variations:***

✏ These shoes make wonderful gifts for parents.

✏ Fill an old tennis shoe with dirt. Plant flower seeds in it, water, and watch it grow.

# YESTERDAY—TODAY—AND TOMORROW

The concept of time is an illusive one for children, but this triarama is a concrete way for them to think about their life—where they have been, where they are, and where they are going.

**You will need:**
three sheets of 9″ × 9″ paper for each child

crayons or markers

stapler

hole punch

yarn or string

scissors

**Directions:**

1. Ask the children what they liked to do when they were babies or toddlers. Next, let them share things they like to do now. Then have them imagine what they will be like when they grow up.

2. Give each child three paper squares. Demonstrate how to fold each in half diagonally; then into fourths.

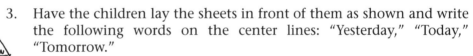

3. Have the children lay the sheets in front of them as shown and write the following words on the center lines: "Yesterday," "Today," "Tomorrow."

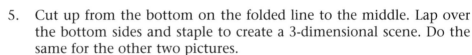

4. Next, ask the children to draw a picture of themselves when they were little on "Yesterday." Have them draw how they look now on "Today," and draw what they think they will be like when they grow up on "Tomorrow." (Remind them to only draw above the center line.)

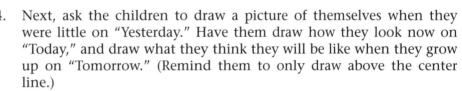

5. Cut up from the bottom on the folded line to the middle. Lap over the bottom sides and staple to create a 3-dimensional scene. Do the same for the other two pictures.

6. Staple the sides of the different scenes together to create a triangular sculpture.

7. Punch a hole in the top where the three sections join and hang from the ceiling.

**Variations:**
- Construct the triarama over a three-day period.
- For younger children, just have them draw one picture of themselves.

# TIMELINE

Here is another activity that will help children focus on how they are growing and changing.

**You will need:**    one sheet of 30″ × 8″ paper

markers or crayons

**Directions:**
1. Several days before starting this project, write the parents a note asking them to send in one photo from each year of their child's life. (Have parents write their child's name and age on the back of each photo.)

2. Draw a line horizontally on the paper. Write the following ages under the line:

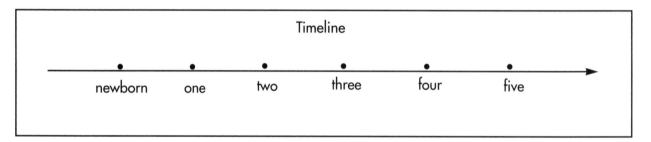

(Adapt the ages to how old your children are.)

3. Ask the children to lay out their photos in front of them to show how they've grown since they were a baby. Encourage the children to talk about how they've changed. "What can you do now that you couldn't do when you were a baby?"

4. Have the children place their pictures on the timeline.

**Variations:**
- Let the children draw their own timelines on long strips of paper. Have them include their date of birth, when they started school, birthdays, holidays, and other special events in their lives. At the far right ask them to draw what they think they'll be like when they grow up.

- Use a timeline to record events in your classroom throughout the year.

# SUPER HEROES

All children need positive heroes they can look up to and model their lives after. This project will give children a positive alternative to the television action figures that are often violent.

**You will need:**

one 12″ × 14″ piece of aluminum foil for each child
fabric scraps
glue
yarn
wiggly eyes
scissors

**Directions:**

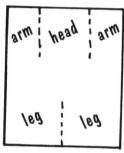

1. Ask the children how they would describe a super hero. Let them suggest several heroes; then evaluate their positive qualities.

2. Give each child a piece of aluminum foil from which to construct their own hero.

3. Make two cuts from the top about one-third of the way down as shown. Make one cut up from the bottom.

4. Squeeze the bottom sections together to make legs. Mold the top sections to make arms, and use the middle section to make a head.

5. Cut a cape from a piece of fabric using the pattern at the bottom of the page.

6. Let the children decorate their hero with wiggly eyes and yarn hair.

7. Have the children name their heroes and tell the class how they help people.

**Variation:**

✏ Let the children work in groups and put on skits with their heroes.

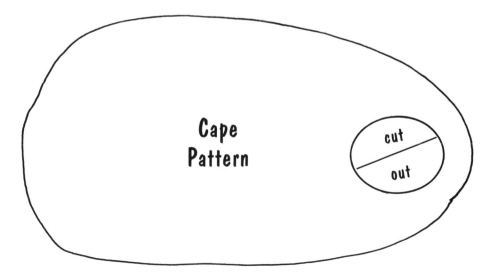

Cape
Pattern

cut
out

233

# IF I COULD CHANGE THE WORLD

Children are often overwhelmed by the "big" world in which they live. This activity will allow them to fantasize their feelings and empower them to make changes in the future.

*You will need:*    chart paper
markers

*Directions:*

1. Print "If I Could Change the World" at the top of the chart.

2. Tell the children to pretend they are a magic genie who can do anything he or she wants. What would they do to change the world and make it a better place?

3. Write each child's name and his or her response on the chart.

4. To conclude, read the list and ask the children "how" they would go about making those changes.

*Variations:*

✏ Have the children write letters to the President, governor, or other politicians about issues impacting them and education.

✏ Try some of these other sentence starters for group stories or individual writing assignments:

If I could change my teacher I would. . .
If I could change my family I would. . .
If I could change myself I would. . .

© 1997 by John Wiley & Sons

> **If I Could Change the World**
>
> Marcus- I would get rid of all the guns.
> Kelly- I would give food to all the poor people.
> Hoa- I'd make all the bad people go to jail.
> Kendra- I'd tell everyone to be friends.

# I WISH I WERE

Giving children wishes will provide you with some interesting insight into their dreams and feelings. This activity will also reinforce the connection between written and spoken language.

**You will need:**

tape recorder
paper, pencils
crayons or markers
construction paper, stapler

**Directions:**

1. Sing this song to the tune of "If You're Happy and You Know It."

   Oh, I wish I were a little race car.
   Oh, I wish I were a little race car.
   I'd go zoom, zoom, zoom,
   All over your room.
   Oh, I wish I were a little race car.

2. Ask the children if they ever wish they were something or someone other than themselves. Let them think for a few minutes about what they would be; then let each child complete this sentence in the tape recorder: "I wish I were _____ because _____."

3. Write each child's name and statement on a piece of paper. Then ask the children to draw a picture to go with it.

4. Put their papers together in the construction paper and staple along the sides to make a book.

5. Read the book with the class and then put it in your classroom library.

**Variation:**

✏ Have the children complete the following statements:

   I wish my teacher would. . .
   I wish my parents would. . .
   I wish my brother/sister would. . .
   I wish my pet would. . .
   I wish my friends would. . .

# DREAM JAR

All children need dreams and hopes. This dream jar will give them a tangible way of verbalizing their inner desires and goals.

**You will need:**
one plastic jar with a lid for each child
glitter
cotton
glue
permanent markers
paper
crayons

**Directions:**
1. Several days before doing this activity, ask each child to bring in a plastic jar with a lid.
2. Have the children close their eyes and relax. Ask them to think about a secret dream they have. Tell them to create a picture of it in their mind.
3. Next, ask the children to open their eyes and draw a picture of their dream.
4. Have each child put his or her dream picture in their jar. They can then decorate the outside of the jar with glitter, cotton, and markers.
5. Encourage the children to take their dream jars home and continue to add their dreams to their jars.

**Variations:**
✏ Have the children dictate a sentence or write a story about their dreams.
✏ Make a class book called "Dream a Dream" in which each child contributes a picture of a dream he or she has.

**Hint:**
Carefully supervise glitter with young children, or substitute with glitter pens.

# FLYING HIGH GOALS

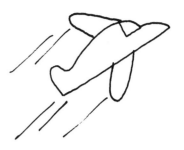

One of the first steps in achieving a goal is writing it down. Children will be encouraged to think about their goals and how they might accomplish them as they have fun making and flying paper airplanes.

**You will need:**

paper
pencils or crayons

**Directions:**

1. Have all the children identify a goal they would like to accomplish within the next several months.

2. Give the children the paper and ask them to write that goal or draw a picture of themselves accomplishing that goal.

3. Show the children how to fold their paper into an airplane according to the directions below.

4. Ask them to explain their goal. Then fly it across the room.

5. Follow up in several months to see who has achieved their goal.

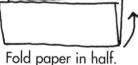

Fold paper in half.

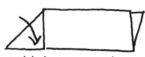

Fold down triangle.

Fold down top to bottom edge.

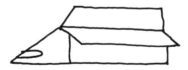

Lift up wings and fly.
(Attach a paper clip to the nose for a greater distance.)

**Variations:**

✎ Do this project at the beginning of the school year by asking the children to set yearly goals.

✎ Discuss the difference between short-term and long-term goals.

# PUPPET PEOPLE

Children will have fun imagining what they will be when they grow up. These puppets will also encourage children to verbalize their goals.

**You will need:**  mirror

magazines or catalogs (provide magazines that reflect different ethnic groups, as well as men and women in different roles)

scissors

craft sticks

tape

**Directions:**

1. Show the children the mirror and tell them to pretend they can look into the future to see what they will be when they grow up.

2. Let each child look in the mirror and describe how they see themselves.

3. Pass out the magazines and ask the children to find a person who represents what they want to be when they grow up. Have them cut out that person and tape it to a stick.

4. Let the children take turns holding up their puppets as they describe what they want to be when they grow up.

**Variations:**

- Have the children put on a puppet show with their stick puppets.
- Make magazine puppets of different kinds of families. Include various ages, sexes, and ethnic groups.

# ALL DRESSED UP

As children put on a fashion show in their parents' clothes, they will be exploring different careers and what they might want to be when they grow up.

**You will need:**  dress-up clothes
career hats and props

**Directions:**

1. Several days before dressing up, ask the children about the jobs their parents do. Let them share what they might want to do when they grow up. Explain that you will have a "dress-up" day when they can come dressed like their parents or the career they want to have when they grow up.

2. Remind the children daily about dressing up, or send home a note to the parents.

3. On dress-up day, let each child get up and describe what he or she wants to be when he or she grows up and why. Extend their language skills by asking what they will do when they have that job. How will they prepare for that career?

4. Take the children on a parade around the school in their dress-up clothes, or put on a fashion show in your classroom.

**Variations:**

✏ Make a video of the children in their costumes. Then play it back for parents at a meeting or conference.

✏ Integrate dress-up day with a unit on community helpers or career education.

✏ Put dress-up clothes and career hats and props in the Dramatic Play area.

✏ Invite parents to talk about their different professions. Try to include a variety of nontraditional careers so the children can see that a woman could be a wallpaper hanger, for example, or a man could be a nurse.

# TIME CAPSULE

As children reflect on the experiences they have had, they will create a special keepsake of their school year.

**You will need:**
one potato chip canister or tennis ball can for each child
construction paper
crayons, glue, scissors, pencils
scrap box

**Directions:**

1. Several weeks before the end of the school year, ask the children to bring in a chip canister or tennis ball can.

2. Let them cover the canisters with construction paper and decorate with crayons. (Make sure they put their name and date on the outside.)

3. Explain what a time capsule is and how people use it to tell future generations about their lives and culture.

4. Review some of the highlights of your school year, asking children to share what they've learned, favorite moments, field trips, celebrations, and so forth.

5. Let the children clean out their desks, cubbies, and other centers in the room and put objects and momentoes in their time capsules. Have them make souvenirs from construction paper or write stories about their friends and experiences.

6. Encourage the children to take their time capsules home on the last day of school and to save them until they grow up.

**Variations:**

✏ Involve the class in making a large time capsule for the school. Date and store the capsule in the school library for future classes.

✏ Start individual time capsules at the beginning of the school year so children can save favorite momentoes, papers, and art projects throughout the year.

# BLAST OFF TO THE FUTURE

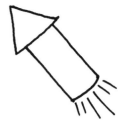

Children will be challenged to think about what they want to do in the future as they blast off to the year 2XXX.

***You will need:***
old clock
gift box
tissue paper
paper, crayons

***Directions:***

1. Wrap up the clock in the tissue paper and put it in the box.

2. Gather the children and tell them that you have a time machine in the box that can take them 20 years into the future. Carefully remove the clock and ask the children if they are ready for their exciting journey. Have the children pretend to climb into a rocket and fasten their seat belts. Tell them to close their eyes as you make a loud booming noise.

3. Have the children open their eyes and pretend they have traveled into the future. Ask the following questions:

   — How old are you?
   — What do you look like?
   — Where do you live?
   — Tell me about your family.
   — What kind of work do you do?
   — How do people travel around?
   — What are some new inventions?

4. Ask the children to close their eyes and travel back to the present time. Conclude by having the children draw pictures about their visit to the future.

***Variations:***

✏ Older children could write stories about a future time in their lives.

✏ Let the children work together on a mural that depicts life at some future time.

241

# 6

# Parent Pack

How true is the saying, "Parents are their child's first and most important teacher!" The partnership between the home and school is a critical one to children and to their academic and emotional success. This section is a resource of ideas for involving parents in your school program. There are also take-home activities that will encourage quality time and help parents enhance their child's self-esteem.

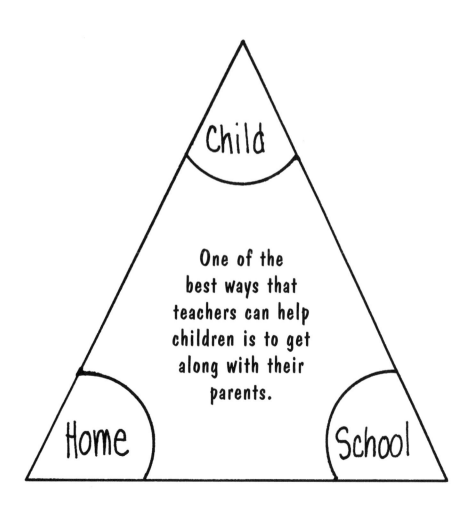

Child

One of the
best ways that
teachers can help
children is to get
along with their
parents.

Home

School

# POSITIVE PARTNERSHIPS

To help children be the best they can be requires commitment from educators and families. Below are some ideas that will nurture a positive relationship.

**_Orientation —_**  Plan an orientation meeting for new families. Include a tour of the building, introductions to staff, an explanation of your philosophy and goals, expectations, etc. Encourage parents to ask questions or to voice concerns.

**_Parent Handbook —_**  Prepare a handbook for each family with a yearly calendar, policies (for illnesses, dress code, discipline, etc.), daily schedules, program descriptions, etc.

**_Parent Advisory Board —_**  Establish a parent advisory board to act as the liaison between families and the school. Use the Board's input in constructing curriculum, making budgets, solving problems, and planning for the future. Another instrumental committee to your school could be a Diversity Committee to guide the school in reflecting various cultures and ethnic groups.

**_Home Visit —_**  Many schools include a home visitation before school starts and at the end of the year. When the teacher visits the home, it lets parents know how much the teacher cares about their child and can give the teacher valuable insight into the child.

**_Videos & Tapes —_**  Make videos or audiotapes of children singing songs, acting out stories, playing in learning centers, participating in an art activity, etc. Allow children to take turns bringing the tapes home to share with their families.

**_Suggestion Box —_**  Keep a suggestion box in your school lobby and remind parents how important their ideas and input are to you.

© 1997 by John Louis Wilson & Sons

**Family Photos —** Display family photos in classrooms, on bulletin boards, or use them to make classroom books.

**Weekly or Monthly Newsletter —** Send home a weekly or monthly newsletter to parents with information about units of study, special events, community activities, words to songs, cooking activities, etc.

**Workshops and Focus Groups —** Offer workshops on issues of concern to families. Bedtime, divorce, sibling rivalry, attention deficit disorders, and stress are several topics that might be discussed by school personnel or outside professionals.

**Observations —** Have an "open door" policy and encourage parents to visit your classroom frequently.

**Open Houses, Field Trips, Work Days, Socials —** Schools are in a unique position to provide social and emotional support for families without relatives close by. Potluck suppers, trips to the zoo, work days, or talent shows are a wonderful way to connect families and the school.

**Plays and Programs —** When children perform, everyone shows up and has a good time!

**Parent Experts —** Use the expertise of your parents to help decorate classrooms, renovate playgrounds, type newsletters, etc.

**Parent Bulletin Boards** Create a special area in each classroom with information useful to parents. A copy of the lesson plan, menu, calendar, pertinent articles, photos of the children, art projects to make at home, or funny sayings from the children could all be posted.

**Listen! Listen! — Listen! —** Take time to really listen to parents. Answer their questions and respond to their individual needs as much as possible.

# CONSTRUCTIVE COMMUNICATION

Keeping communication open and frequent is another positive way to build parent partnerships.

**Phone Calls —**

Call parents with "good news" about their child's progress or to share a "special moment."

**Daily Notes/Weekly Notes —**

Send daily or weekly notes home to parents to let them know how their child is doing at school. The individual attention will certainly be appreciated.

**Activity Calendars —**

Prepare a weekly or monthly calendar of projects or learning activities parents can do at home with their children. (See the sample on page 247.)

**Portfolios —**

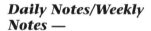

Keep an ongoing portfolio for each child in your room. These are an excellent way to show parents what their children "can do" at conference time. (See the sample on page 248.)

**Conferences —**

Plan several conferences during the school year to discuss children's development, set goals, resolve concerns, etc. Use the questionnaire on page 249 to gain information about the children and get feedback from the parents.

**Picture Me! —**

Each month or quarter fill out a "Picture Me" sheet on each child. (See the sample on page 250.) Send one copy home and save one for the child's portfolio. This can also be a valuable tool to help you observe individual children.

# PLAY WITH ME
## ACTIVITY CALENDAR

| SUNDAY | MONDAY | TUESDAY | WEDNESDAY | THURSDAY | FRIDAY | SATURDAY |
|---|---|---|---|---|---|---|
|  | Sing a song together. | Make something for dinner together. | How many people are in your family? Draw a picture of them. | Go on a shape hunt. Can you find a △ ○ □ ? | Take a walk at night. What can you see? hear? smell? | Call a friend to come and play. |
| Give someone a hug. | Look at some of your baby pictures. How have you changed? | Do some exercises together. | Look in the mirror. What do you like about yourself? | Say some nursery rhymes. | Play a game together. | Make a "super duper" sandwich and share it. |
| Go outside and look for something beautiful. | Talk about what you did at school today. | Work a puzzle together. | Make a wish. | Freeze orange juice in a paper cup with a stick to make an ice pop. | Sing the alphabet song. | Do a job around the house. |
| Tell someone you love him or her. | Run, jump, hop, gallop, and skip. | Read a book. | Take pretzel sticks and pretzel twists. Make letters and numerals with them. | Throw a ball. | Think of words that rhyme. | Play Hide-and-Seek. |
| Write a letter to your grandparents. | Tell a joke. | Trace around your hand and foot. What can you make out of them? | Take a walk in your neighborhood. Find a pretty rock. | Count as high as you can. |  |  |

247

# Building Portfolios for Children

A portfolio enables teachers to provide an ongoing "picture" of a child's development. A portfolio shows what a child knows and can do, rather than what a child can't do. Further, a portfolio supports a developmental philosophy about how children learn by reflecting social, emotional, physical, and cognitive growth.

Create a portfolio for each child at the beginning of the school year. Store portfolios in a filing box and add to them throughout the year. This will be a special "remembrance" the children can take with them at the end of the year.

Below are a few examples you may want to include in a child's portfolio:

self portraits

art projects

writing samples (scribbles, journals, stories)

anecdotal records (funny sayings, special moments)

photographs

dictated stories

summary of parent conferences

interest inventory ("Picture Me")

assessment sheets

teacher observations

work samples (cutting, math activities)

other meaningful information

# PARENT CONFERENCE QUESTIONNAIRE

Please complete the statements below and bring this with you when you come for our conference. I'll look forward to the insight you will share with me about your child.

Child's Name _____ Date _____

1. My child's favorite activity at school is _____

_____

2. My child expresses concern about _____

_____

3. My child's strong qualities are _____

_____

4. Areas I feel my child needs to work on are _____

_____

5. Something my child would like to do at school is _____

_____

6. Something I would like to see my child do at school is _____

_____

7. Is there any special information about your child that you think we should know

about? _____

_____

_____

_____

_____

# PICTURE ME!

Child's Name _____     Date _____

My favorite things to do are. . .

My special friends are. . .

Books I like to read are. . .

A song I like to sing is. . .

I like to eat. . .

My favorite center is. . .

What I like best about school is. . .

Attach a picture the child has drawn
of himself or herself.

This is me on _____.

# LEARNING BAGS

Parents an help reinforce concepts children are learning at school with these bags. They will also help parents become more aware of skills their child needs to work on.

***You will need:***   one paper lunch bag for each child
markers

***Directions:***

1. Print a different numeral (from 2 through 10) on each bag. Make one for each child in the room.

2. Before dismissing the children, explain that you have some special homework for them to do. Pass out a bag to each child and tell them to find a set of objects around their house that matches the numeral on their bag.

3. Let the children share what they have found in small groups at school the next day.

4. Put all the objects together and use them for sorting, counting, patterning, and other math activities.

***Variations:***

✏ Send a letter home to parents explaining the purpose of learning bags.

✏ Use learning bags to reinforce these other concepts:

*Shapes* — Draw shapes on bags and have children bring in that shape.

*Colors* — Mark bags with different colors of crayons and tell children to bring in something that color.

*Letters* — Print letters on bags and have children find objects that start with that sound.

*Words* — Ask children to cut out words and labels they can read and put them in the bag.

*Signs of Seasons* — Have children bring in a "sign of fall," "sign of winter," etc.

*Senses* — Ask children to bring in objects they like to see, hear, smell, touch, or taste.

# COUNT-AT-HOME BOOK

Parents and children will get involved together as they count objects around the house.

**You will need:**   8″ × 10″ construction paper
markers or crayons
two book rings
laminator or clear self-stick vinyl
erasable marking pen
hole punch

**Directions:**

1. Prepare a book similar to the one below by drawing common household objects on the construction paper.

2. Laminate or cover with clear self-stick vinyl. Punch two holes in the side of each page and put them together with book rings.

3. Allow one child to take the book home each evening with an erasable marker.

4. Let that child share their results at school the next day.

# I CAN READ!

Reading skills will be reinforced as children recognize environmental print.

**You will need:**

posterboard (cut in half)

magazines, newspapers advertisements, food labels

markers

scissors, glue

**Directions:**

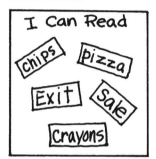

1. Give each child half a sheet of posterboard. Let the children copy "I Can Read" on their poster. (An adult may need to write this for younger children.)

2. Have the children cut out words they can read from magazines, newspapers, and food labels and glue them on the poster.

3. Send home the poster with a note to the parents similar to the one below.

Dear Parents:

Learning to recognize signs, labels, and familiar print in their environment is a first step in learning how to read. Hang this poster with words your child can recognize on your refrigerator. Then encourage your child to add to it by cutting out or writing other words they can read. (Food wrappers, logos, and street signs are a few suggestions.) When you fill up this poster, start another one.

Thanks for your support!

**Variation:**

⬧ Have children make posters to reinforce other concepts you are working on such as letter recognition, numerals, colors, etc.

# TAG-ALONG TEDDY

**You will need:**
cloth bag or backpack
teddy bear or other stuffed animal
notebook, pen, crayons

**Directions:**

1. Have the children suggest names for the teddy bear. Explain that each night a different friend will get to take home the bear and tell a story about his or her adventures.

2. Place the bear, notebook, pen, and crayons in the bag along with a letter similar to the one below.

Dear Parents:

Today your child is bringing home our class teddy bear. Please let your child dictate a story to you about his or her adventures with the bear. Write the story in the notebook; then let your child color a picture to go along with it. Tomorrow we will read your child's story to the class.

Thanks for helping our children get interested in reading and writing by participating in this project.

Sincerely,

3. Read the child's story to the class on the following day.

**Variations:**

✎ Add a storybook, toothbrush, change of clothes, or other objects for the teddy bear to extend imaginative play.

✎ Older children could take turns writing their own stories about adventures with a stuffed animal.

**Hint:**
Be prepared to let children dictate a story to you if their parents do not participate.

# BAG A BOOK

One of the most effective ways parents can help their children at home is to read to them. These book bags are a perfect way to put a book in parents' hands, plus they will have a follow-up activity to do.

**You will need:**  children's books (purchase these at thrift stores, yard sales, used book-stores, or ask parents to donate old books)

large ziplock bags

4″ × 6″ index cards

**Directions:**

1. Prepare an index card with a follow-up activity for each book. You might use a finger play, song, cooking activity, art project, game, etc.

2. Put books and activity cards into ziplock bags.

3. Allow children to check out a different book bag each week.

**Variations:**

- ✏ Let parents check out other classroom toys and games.

- ✏ Have a workshop for parents to make games and learning materials to use at home with their children.

- ✏ Get together with a group of teachers to brainstorm activities to put on follow-up cards. Rotate book bags with other classes.

# HOMEWORK TASK CARDS

These cards provide another way to extend learning at home and involve parents in your school program.

**You will need:**

4" × 6" cards

felt-tip markers

**Directions:**

1. Prepare homework task cards similar to the ones on the following pages. Write a different activity on each index card, adapting them to your students' abilities and interests.

2. Allow children to check out a different homework card each evening.

3. Have the children write their names on the backs of the cards after they have completed the activity.

**Variations:**

✏ Add new cards to keep parents and children interested.

✏ Decorate the cards with pictures or stickers.

✏ Keep a graph of the activities the children have completed.

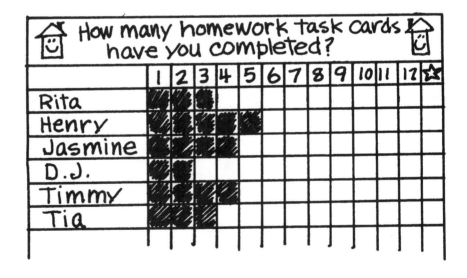

# HOMEWORK ACTIVITIES FOR CHILDREN AND PARENTS*

1.  Read a story together.
2.  Draw a picture of what you did at school today and tell someone in your family about it.
3.  How many objects in your house use electricity?
4.  Teach your family a song.
5.  Cook something for dinner.
6.  Take a walk with someone in your family.
7.  Count the money in your piggy bank.
8.  Watch the weather report.
9.  Play a board game.
10. Make a puppet from a paper lunch bag.
11. Find 8 objects in your house that are black.
12. Count the number of shoes in your house.
13. Plan a dream vacation.
14. Fold the laundry and sort it by who it belongs to.
15. Ask your parents to tell you what they liked to do when they were your age.
16. Find 10 objects that you can hold in the palm of your hand.
17. Go around the house and find labels you can read.
18. Count the trees in your yard. What else can you count in your yard?
19. Look for different shapes around your house.
20. Say some nursery rhymes. Can you make up one of your own?
21. Make up your own bedtime story tonight.
22. Make a wish upon a star tonight. Have your family make a wish, too.
23. Cut out magazine pictures of foods you like to eat and glue them on a paper plate.
24. Plan a family celebration.
25. Do some exercises together.
26. Tell jokes and riddles to each other.
27. Wad up a pair of socks. Practice throwing it in a box or basket.
28. Watch a television program with your family. Then tell each other what you liked or disliked about it.
29. Cut out coupons from the newspaper. How much money can you save?

---

* Adapt these activities to your curriculum and your students' skills.

# HOMEWORK ACTIVITIES *(continued)*

30. Look for objects in your house that start with each letter of the alphabet.

31. Cut the front off a cereal box. Cut it into a puzzle; then try to put it back together.

32. Go on a seed hunt in your kitchen. How many foods can you find with seeds?

33. Get cereal or pasta with a hole in the middle and string it on yarn or dental floss to make a necklace.

34. Read the newspaper comics together.

35. Play "I Spy."

36. Give a back rub to someone in your family.

37. How many things in your house use batteries?

38. Learn to say something in a different language.

39. Go outside tonight and look at the moon. What shape is it? How many stars can you count?

40. Ask your parents to tell you what you were like when you were a baby.

41. Play "Simon Says."

42. How many things in your house can you sit on?

43. Draw a picture or write a letter to someone you love.

44. Make a pattern using shoes and socks. For example, shoe, shoe, sock, shoe, shoe, sock.

45. Name five things you can wear when it's cold outside.

46. How many things in your home come from trees?

47. Count by 2's, 5's, and 10's.

48. Draw a map of your neighborhood.

49. Finish the sentence, "I wish I were _____."

50. How many days are in the week? Can you name them?

51. How many months are there? Can you name them?

52. Find a picture in the newspaper or a magazine and make up a story about it.

53. Get a book and tell a family member the author and illustrator.

54. Act out these opposites: *hot* and *cold; up* and *down; in* and *out; fast* and *slow; loud* and *quiet.*

55. Recite your address and phone number to your parents.

56. Think of words that rhyme with "tall," "cake," "man," "bike," "run," and "it."

57. Play "Hide-and-Seek."

58. Ask your parents to teach you a poem.

59. Find something in your kitchen you can use or play like a musical instrument.

60. Draw a picture of what you want to be when you grow up and tell a family member about it.

# "SCHOOL IS FUN" BOOK

**This book will help parents understand developmentally appropriate practices and the value of play in the lives of their children.**

*You will need:*   9″ × 12″ construction paper
school supply magazines
scissors
glue
stapler

*Directions:*

1. Make a cover for the book called "School Is Fun."

2. On each page, cut out an appropriate picture from the school supply magazine and write one of the captions given on the following page.

3. Staple the pages together to make a book.

4. Read the book to the class. Then allow one child to take the book home each day.

*Variations:*

✏ Take photos of the children playing in the various centers in the classroom and use these to illustrate the different pages.

✏ Let the children draw pictures to illustrate the centers in the book.

✏ Invite parents for a "play time." Let them paint, build with blocks, work puzzles, or play in housekeeping. Then parents should reflect on all the skills children are developing as they play.

# SCHOOL IS FUN!

(Use children's drawings, photos of the children, or pictures from school supply catalogs to illustrate the pages in this book.)

*Blocks*

In the Block Center,
I'm learning skills that
I may use one day as
an architect or city planner.

*Language*

The Language Center is getting me
ready for a lifetime of reading.

*Science*

In the Science Center, I'm
experimenting and discovering.
I may use these skills as a chemist
or biologist when I grow up.

*Library*

When I go to the library, I'm
learning to love books.

*Manipulative*

Manipulative materials develop my
small muscles and build skills I
may use one day as a surgeon.

*Large Motor*

When I use my large muscles, I'm
releasing energy and learning skills
I may use as a professional athlete.

**Remember:** Play *is* a child's work!

I hear and I forget—
   I see and I remember—
      I do and I understand!
          *—Chinese Proverb*

*Dramatic Play/Housekeeping*

In the Dramatic Play Center,
I'm learning how to be a mommy,
daddy, doctor, or police officer.

*Art*

At the Art Center, I'm expressing
myself creatively and learning skills
I may use as a painter or sculptor.

*Writing*

At the Writing Center, I'm
developing skills I may use as an
author or journalist.

*Math*

In the Math Center, I'm learning
concepts that may help me become
an accountant or computer
programmer.

*Music*

At the Music Center, I'm learning
how to become a conductor or
musician.

# WHO IS MY TEACHER?

Being a "real person" to parents and children is so important. This book will be a great way to show them your personal side.

**You will need:**
personal photos (as a child, your family, your parents, enjoying hobbies, etc.)

construction paper

markers

stapler

**Directions:**

1. Prepare a book with personal information about yourself before the beginning of the school year. You might include:

   — where you were born

   — baby photo

   — photos from your school days

   — photos of your family, pets, hobbies, and sports you enjoy

   — favorite foods

   — why you enjoy teaching

   — fun activities the class will do at school this year

2. Glue a photo or draw a picture on each page. Then staple the book together.

3. Share the book with the class on the first day of school. Let one child each night take the book home to show to his or her family.

**Variation:**

✏ Write a letter about yourself and send it to each child before the school year begins.

# ART PORTFOLIO

This take-home box of art materials will be a positive suggestion to parents of simple materials they can provide for their children to foster creativity.

**You will need:**    detergent box with a handle (a cloth bag, backpack, or old briefcase can also be used)

art materials such as crayons, chalk, colored pencils, scissors, tape, markers, glue, scrap paper, watercolors, pipe cleaners, clay, hole punch, lunch bags, paper plates, cardboard rollers, envelopes, etc.

**Directions:**

1. Decorate the outside of the box by making a collage on it. (The children would probably enjoy helping you do this.)

2. Fill the box with the above art materials.

3. Select one child each day to be the "artist" and take home the art portfolio.

4. Ask the children to share what they made the following day when they return the art box to school.

**Variations:**

- Make a *math kit* with felt shapes, magnetic numerals, a tape measure, ruler, minute timer, play coins, and objects to sort and count.

- Create a *writing portfolio* with scrap paper, sticky notes, pens, pencils, envelopes, junk mail, notepads, etc.

- Construct a *science kit* with a magnet, magnifying glass, flashlight, paper, pencils, shells, rocks, bones, and other interesting objects.

# PARENT RESOURCE LIBRARY

Create a parent resource library for your school to provide support and helpful information for families.

**You will need:**
parenting books (ages and stages, sibling rivalry, positive communication, etc.)

pertinent articles on parenting (bedtime, single parenting, death, ADD/ADHD, health issues, etc.)

audio- and videotapes on parenting topics

bookshelf

table

**Directions:**

1. Place the books and tapes on a shelf in your library or school office. Articles can be organized by topic and stored in a file box.

2. Ask parents to write their name when checking out materials.

**Variations:**

✏ Involve parents in creating the resource center by sharing books or articles that have been helpful to them.

✏ Copy articles to send home to parents on issues they express concerns about.

# SPOTLIGHT

Parents will be encouraged to focus on their child's unique personality and strengths as they write a description about them. And won't children feel loved and special by the descriptions their parents have written about them!

**You will need:**  copy of a letter for each parent
envelope

**Directions:**
1. Send home a copy of a letter similar to the one below asking each parent to write a description of his or her child.

> Dear Parents:
>
> We are going to play a game called "Spotlight" at school and we need your help. Would you please write a description of your child without using your child's name? You might include a physical description, likes and dislikes, things the child is good at, favorite sayings, or other information that makes your child special. Please seal the description in the attached envelope so your child doesn't see it and return it to school.
>
> We will read each of these "Spotlights" in class and see if your child can guess which one describes him or her.
>
> We really appreciate your help! Thank you.
>
> Sincerely,

2. Read all the descriptions to the children. See if they can identify which "Spotlight" described them.

**Variations:**
- Make a bulletin board with each child's photo and the description.
- Put the descriptions together to make a class book.

**Hint:**  Be prepared to write a description for children whose parents don't participate.

# FEATURED FAMILY

Both children and parents will have fun creating this poster about their family. They will all be proud to see it displayed in the classroom.

**You will need:**   copy of letter for each family
posterboard
marker

**Directions:**

1. Select one family each week to be highlighted. Print their name on the posterboard.

2. Let the child take home the posterboard, along with the letter on the following page the weekend before the family is highlighted.

3. Have children share their poster with classmates on Monday morning. Then hang the poster in a prominent place in the classroom.

4. Give the children their poster to take home at the end of the week, or display them permanently on a wall in the hall or classroom.

**Variation:**   ✏ Keep a special bulletin board in the classroom where children can display their family photos.

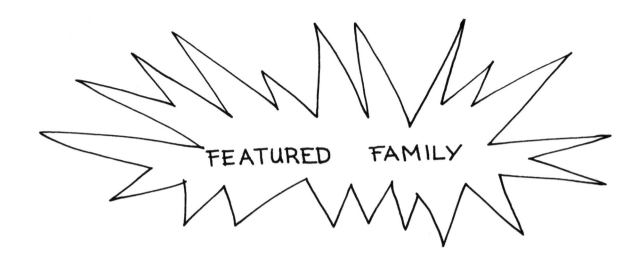

FEATURED FAMILY

Dear _____,

Congratulations! You have been selected to be our featured family for next week. This is our way of giving some special attention to your child, while helping us to get to know you better. Please work with your child to decorate the poster with photos of your family, pets, special celebrations, and traditions. Also, encourage your child to draw some pictures on the poster of your home, family members, hobbies, or how you have fun together. We'll let your child share the poster on Monday and tell a little about your family. Then we'll hang the poster in the room next week. Your child can take it home next Friday to save as a special memory.

Thanks for sharing with us. How proud your child will be of his or her "featured family!"

Sincerely,

# BOX OF LOVE

These little notes will be a tangible way to help children and parents express their love for each other and will promote quality family time.

**You will need:**
tissue box or other small box

construction paper, magazines, paint, stickers, fabric scraps, and other collage materials

scissors

glue

one copy of idea cards for each child (see following page)

**Directions:**

1. Let the children decorate their boxes with the art materials.

2. Give each child a copy of the idea cards and have them cut them apart along the dotted lines. (An adult may need to do this for young children.)

3. Have the children insert their cards in their boxes.

4. Tell the children to pull out a note each day and do it with their parents. Or send a letter home to the parents explaining the purpose of the "box of love."

**Variations:**

✎ Encourage the families to save the idea cards and use them over again. Or suggest they create their own idea cards of favorite activities.

✎ Ask older children to make their own activity cards for their "box of love."

✎ Send home monthly idea cards in newsletters with recipes, art projects, words to songs, and other fun things families can do together.

Play Dough
2 cups flour
1 cup salt
2 cups water
2 T. oil
1 tsp. cream of tarter

Little Red Box
I wish I had a
little red box
to put my
money in.

Nature Bracelet
Put a piece of
tape around your
child's wrist with
the sticky side out.

# IDEA CARDS

IG hug?

Please read me a story.

Let's sing a song together.

Would you like to go for a walk?

A back rub at bedtime
sure would feel good.

Play a game with me.

Tell me what you
like about me.

I Am
Special

Let's cook something together.

# MY GOOD BOOK

Parents will focus on their child's positive qualities with this book, and the child's self-concept will be enhanced. It will also nurture reading and writing skills.

**You will need:**

18″ × 12″ construction paper
8-1/2″ × 11″ paper
stapler
crayons or markers
letter to parents

**Directions:**

1.  Make a book for each child by stapling 10 to 20 sheets of paper in the construction paper.

2.  Print the child's name and "Good Book" on the cover. Then let them decorate it with crayons or markers.

3.  Ask the children to draw a picture of something "good" about themselves on the first page. Then have them dictate a sentence to you about it.

4.  Send the book home to the parents along with a note similar to the one on the following page.

**Variation:**

✏ Use a "good book" for journal writing at school.

Dear Parents,

Today your child is bringing home a "good book." Think about all the special qualities your child has; then write them down in the book. Your child may want to draw pictures or glue photos in the books, too. Continue adding to the book when your child does something that makes you feel proud. Read the book when your child is going through a difficult time. Children love to hear "good" things about themselves and will treasure this book and the positive comments you make to them.

You're doing a "good" job, too!

Sincerely,

# I CAN! I CAN

Dear Parents:

Below are directions for a fun activity you can do [...]
you focus on all of your child's positive qualities a[...]
she *can do*.

**You will need:**   a juice can or similar container with a smooth edge
paper
glue
scissors
crayons
strips of paper cut to fit inside the can

**Directions:**

1. Cover the can with paper.

2. Write "I Can" on the can. Then let your child decorate it with crayons.

3. Let your child dictate all of the things he or she can do. Write each one on a strip of paper and let your child place it in the can. (You might include things such as, "I can say my phone number," "I can gallop," "I can brush my teeth," and so forth.)

4. As your child accomplishes new tasks, write them on a strip of paper and add them to the can.

5. Continue this project for several months, reading the strips with your child so he or she can see how much he or she is growing and learning.

This is one you "can do" together!

Sincerely,

# HELPER POUCH

Dear Parents:

Your child will be eager to work around the house with this "helper pouch." When children do chores they develop responsibility and feel a sense of self-worth.

**You will need:**    two paper plates
scissors
stapler
3-inch squares of paper
crayons or markers
magnet or yarn

**Directions:**

1. Cut one paper plate in half. Lay it on top of the other plate and staple them together to make a pocket.

2. Let your child decorate the paper plate pouch with markers or crayons.

3. Ask your child to name some jobs he or she would like to help with around the house. Write these jobs on the squares of paper and put them in the pouch.

4. Use a magnet to attach the helper pouch to your refrigerator, or tie on a piece of yarn so you can hang it on a wall.

5. Each day let your child select a different job to do. (You can also let your child choose a job to do for the whole week.)

Remember to praise your child for a job well done!

Sincerely,

# SWEET DREAMS

Dear Parents,

Do you have a special bedtime ritual that you follow every night when you put your child to bed? How important those little rituals are to giving children security and quality time!

Below are three important questions you might want to include in your bedtime routine. They will help reaffirm your child and give him or her positive thoughts through the night.

Tell me something you did today that made you feel proud.

Tell me something nice you did for someone today.

Tell me something you're looking forward to tomorrow.

Sweet dreams!

**Hint:**   Have your child ask *you* the above questions after they've answered them.

# FAMILY TREES

Dear Parents:

Here is a project you can do with your child called a "family tree." Your child will be proud of his or her special family and all the people who love him or her. Please return the finished tree to school in the next several days so we can hang it in our classroom.

***You will need:***      crayons
tree trunk sheet

***Directions:***

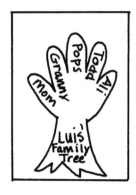

1.   Write your child's name on the tree trunk on the attached page.
2.   Have your child lay his or her hand at the top of the trunk as illustrated to make branches on the tree. Trace around the handprint.
3.   Let your child name different family members as you write them on the branches.
4.   Have your child decorate the tree with crayons.

(If you have a large family, you may need to use two hands to make the branches.)

Thanks for your "hand" in this project!

Sincerely,

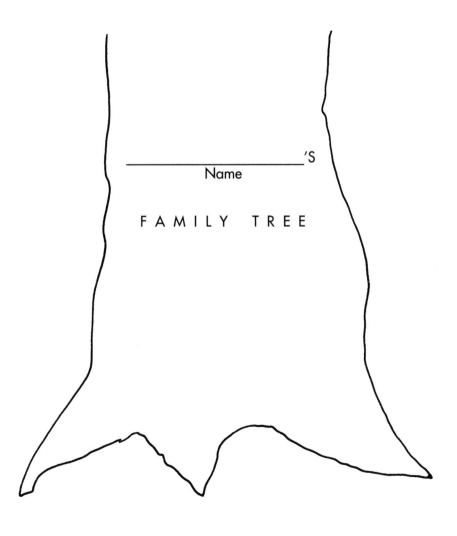

_____'S

Name

FAMILY TREE

# COAT OF ARMS

This project will foster family pride as children and parents work together to create their own coat of arms.

**You will need:**
construction paper, tagboard, or posterboard
markers, crayons
glue, scissors
magazine pictures, photos
shield pattern

**Directions:**

1. Cut out a coat of arms from construction paper, tagboard, or posterboard using the pattern on the following page. (Enlarge it if you desire.)

2. Send home the pattern with each child along with a note to the parents similar to the one below.

---

Dear Parents:

Being a part of a family gives children roots and a sense of belonging. As you decorate the attached coat of arms with your child, you will also be contributing to his or her sense of family pride.

You might want to use photos, magazine pictures, or crayons on your shield. Include things that make your family unique and special, things that you like to do together, or something that represents your culture. Use your imagination!

Please have your child bring the shield back to school in a week so we can hang it in our classroom.

I hope you'll enjoy doing this project together.

Sincerely,

---

**Variation:**

✏ Cut out flag shapes or pennants for children to decorate with their parents.

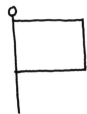
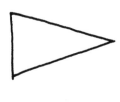

# PATTERN FOR THE COAT OF ARMS

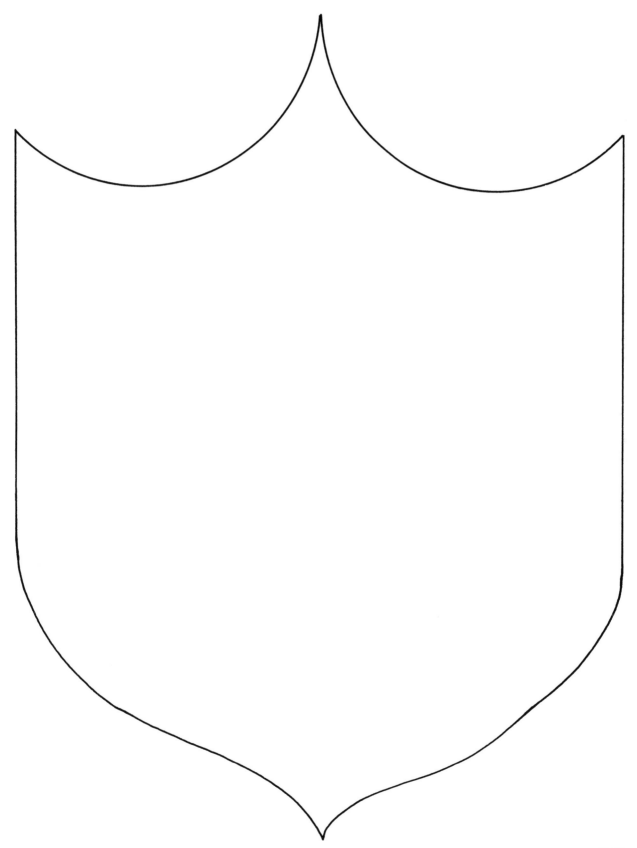

# NOTES

 # NOTES

# NOTES

# NOTES

# NOTES

# NOTES

# NOTES

# NOTES